Discovering Edinburgh

Discovering Edinburgh

KATE VINCENT

Richard Drew Publishing Ltd
20 Park Circus
Glasgow G3 6BE
Scotland

First Published by
Richard Drew Publishing Ltd 1981
The Molendinar Press
20 Park Circus, Glasgow G3 6BE

Copyright © Kate Vincent 1981

ISBN 0 904002 68 3

Made and Printed in Great Britain by
William Collins Sons & Co. Ltd., Glasgow

To

JONATHAN

for whom I discovered Edinburgh

ACKNOWLEDGEMENTS

This book hardly would have been possible without the marvellous resources of the Edinburgh Room of the Central Library and the unfailing helpfulness of its staff.

The maps in this book were drawn by Lorna MacDougall.

CONTENTS

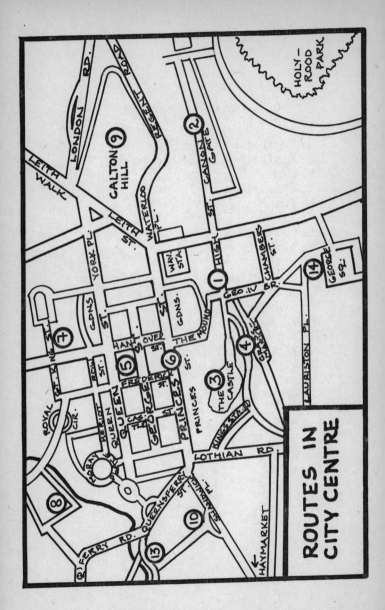

ROUTES IN CITY CENTRE

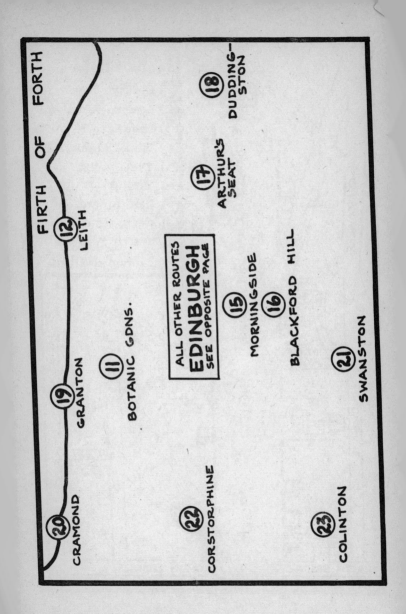

FIRTH OF FORTH

CRAMOND ⑳

⑲ GRANTON

⑫ LEITH

BOTANIC GDNS.

⑪

ALL OTHER ROUTES
EDINBURGH
SEE OPPOSITE PAGE

⑰ ARTHUR'S SEAT

⑱ DUDDING—STON

⑮ MORNINGSIDE

⑯ BLACKFORD HILL

㉑ SWANSTON

CORSTORPHINE ㉒

COLINTON ㉓

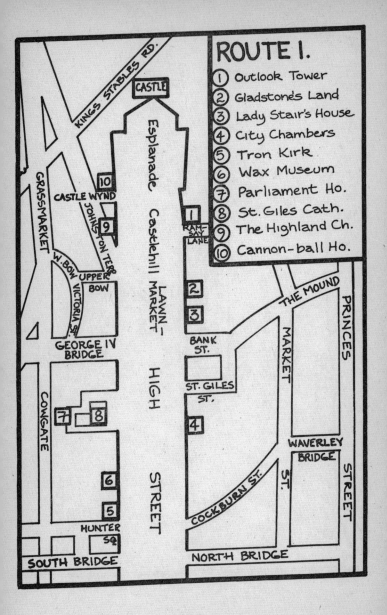

ROUTE I.

1. Outlook Tower
2. Gladstones Land
3. Lady Stair's House
4. City Chambers
5. Tron Kirk
6. Wax Museum
7. Parliament Ho.
8. St. Giles Cath.
9. The Highland Ch.
10. Cannon-ball Ho.

Route 1

THE ROYAL MILE – CASTLE END

In 1724 Daniel Defoe, author of *Robinson Crusoe,* proclaimed the street now known as the Royal Mile to be, 'perhaps the largest, longest and finest street for buildings and number of inhabitants not in Britain only, but in the world.' Times have moved on since then but the Royal Mile, as the backbone of the old city, remains the most fascinating and remarkable street in Edinburgh. There is so much to see, so many stories to tell, that I have divided the Royal Mile into two separate walks. Those with less time to spare however can combine the walks as one.

The best place to begin a walk down the Royal Mile is at the top of Castlehill in the shadow of the castle. In this way, we can follow the development of Edinburgh as it spread from the Castle eastwards, on a rocky ridge formed by the Ice Age. Castlehill is the first street in the Royal Mile which really comprises five different streets.

With your back to the castle, walk on the left-hand side of the road past the curious set of buildings called Ramsay Garden. These were built in the 1890s at the instigation of Sir Patrick Geddes, the 'father of Town-planning', who wanted to persuade 'respectable' people back to the Old Town from the New Town where they were migrating in large numbers. This he hoped would ensure a better social balance in the area. The houses were built around Ramsay Lodge where the poet and author Allan Ramsay lived in the 18th century. Much to Ramsay's irritation the house was nicknamed, 'Goose Pie' because of its octagonal shape.

Ramsay Lane gives a fine view down onto the

Mound and Princes Street, while across the road at the Outlook Tower it is possible to climb the stairs to see the Camera Obscura. Here, weather permitting, the history of the city is told as images of Edinburgh revolve on a concave table. The first Camera Obscura was installed here in the 1850s by Mrs Short although it was later used as a sociological museum by Sir Patrick Geddes. In 1945 better optics were installed and the building re-opened to the public as a Camera Obscura.

Passing Semple's Close, we come to the long building of the General Assembly Hall of the Church of Scotland. On this site was once the Palace of Mary of Guise, the mother of Mary, Queen of Scots. The dark stone of the hall, built by William Playfair between 1836–50, fits in well with its surroundings although the building, from this side at least, is not very distinguished.

We are now in the second street in the Royal Mile, the Lawnmarket, named after the linen market which used to be held here. It is worth going into Milne's Court which, when it was built in the 1690s was the first courtyard, as opposed to a close, to be built in the city – in an attempt to introduce some space into the over-crowded area. Reconstructed in 1971 it is now used as University halls of residence. Steps lead down towards the Mound and from these you can look back and appreciate the height of the tenements which in the Old Town frequently rose above 10 storeys. James Court next door, once provided homes for the philosopher David Hume and James Boswell, the famous biographer of Dr Johnson.

One of the most interesting houses on the Royal Mile is Gladstone's Land. The name of this building may be misleading, 'land' means a tenement block of flats while 'Gladstone' refers not to the famous Victorian Prime Minister but to Thomas Gledstanes who in 1617 extended the house, dating from 1550, to its present size. Now open as a National Trust house, its arcaded front, a common feature of 16th and 17th century Scottish architecture, is the only example of its kind left in Edinburgh.

Lady Stair's Close is worth investigating for the sake of Lady Stair's House which now houses a fine collection of manuscripts and effects relating to Scotland's most famous literary men, Robert Burns, Sir Walter Scott and Robert Louis Stevenson. Originally built in the 17th century, the house was largely rebuilt between 1896–7 and now the only original part is the tower where you can see the initials of the first owners carved above the door. The house and court were named after Elizabeth, widow of the First Earl of Stair, and a noted leader of fashion in her day.

Noticing the unusual dragon-like carvings above the entrance to Wardrop's Court, cross Bank Street, named after the Head Office of the Bank of Scotland standing at the far end. Passing by the rather uninspiring Sheriff Court we come to St Giles' Street which contains the offices of the famous law publishers, W. Green & Son. This takes you into the High Street. Resist the temptation to investigate St Giles' Cathedral for we will come to this on our return. Instead go down Advocates Close and stop on the steps for a fine view of the Scott Monument framed in the middle of the picture. Notice the lintels (stones above the door), and inscriptions on the right.

The imposing City Chambers were originally built as the Royal Exchange in 1761 but the merchants preferred to continue trading in the streets. It soon passed into municipal use and now contains the main offices of Edinburgh District Council. Designed by the Adam Brothers, 1753–1761, it is a fine neoclassical building with elegantly proportioned arches and balconies. Before leaving notice the statue of

13

Alexander and his horse, Bucephalus. Modelled in 1832, the statue originally stood in St Andrew's Square.

You are now in the High Street and the heart of old Edinburgh. Notice the sheer number of closes many of which are now shut up. The way so many closes, courts and wynds (lanes) lead off at right angles from the Royal Mile have reminded many of the bones running across the backbone of a herring skeleton. To complete the skeleton the Castle has been seen as its head, Holyrood Palace as its tail.

If time permits it is worth going into Geddes Close to see a close which still retains a genuine residential feel. A couple of shops after this close keep your eyes peeled for a plaque on the wall marking the site of Gillespie's snuff shop. A generous benefactor to the city, it was suggested that a school which Gillespie endowed should have a new motto, 'who would hae thocht it, that noses had bocht it?' This was presumably a reference to the snuff which was the basis of Gillespie's fortune, but looking at the picture on the plaque it seems that the joke could have as easily applied to Gillespie's own, not inconsiderable, nose!

Fleshmarket Close, named after the Fleshmarket to which it used to lead in the 18th century takes us to Cockburn Street. Named after the famous judge and writer Lord Cockburn, this street was cut through the Old Town in 1866 to provide easier access to and from Waverley Station. We now come to North Bridge, the half-way stage of our walk. If you wish to continue down the Royal Mile turn to page 21.

Walking back up the Royal Mile we come to the Tron Kirk, named after the 'tron' or weighing machine which used to stand nearby. In 1785 a bay had to be cut off the left of the church to make way for the new South Bridge and so for the sake of symmetry a bay was taken off the other side. The stone spire replaces an earlier wooden one burnt down in 1824 while the church's exterior has been recently restored. It is hoped that the church, popular as a rallying point at Hogmanay, will one day re-open as a tourist exhibition centre.

New Assembly Close leads to New Assemblies Hall, once the site of grand dances and now the home of the Wax Museum. The atmosphere of this fine Georgian house is heightened by the sight of elegantly costumed wax figures through the windows.

Covenant Close used to contain a copy of the National Covenant, protesting against the introduction of bishops to Scottish churches, for people to sign; whilst Old Assembly Close is worth investigating for its interesting tradesmen's signs. A little further up, Fishmarket Close is no longer the 'stinking ravine' which an 18th century fishmarket made it.

Notice the curiously designed cobble stones in the street at this point, these mark the site of the old Mercat Cross, dating from the 14th century but demolished except for a shaft, or pillar in 1756. In 1886 the cross, containing the original shaft, was put in its present position a few yards from its first site. Once the scene of everything from trade to executions, Royal Proclamations are still read here occasionally but always 6 days later than in London. This despite our mechanised times is to allow for the journey of the horse-rider from London. The cross itself is the subject of the legend recorded by Scott in his poem, *Marmion*, that before the disastrous Battle of Flodden in 1513 ghostly figures were seen in the city, and from the Mercat Cross came a terrible voice naming those who were to die in the forthcoming battle.

Mercat Cross takes us into Parliament Square, the heart of legal Edinburgh, to the left of the High Street. The square was cast in its present form in the early 19th century by the architect Robert Reid and his attempts to recreate the classical feel of the New Town met with a mixed reaction. Passing the Edinburgh District Court we come to Parliament Hall, built between 1631–40, and occupied by the Scottish Parliament from 1637 to the Union with England in 1707 when the Parliament became largely redundant. Its exterior was redesigned by Reid in 1810 and it is now used for legal purposes. It was here that Sir Walter Scott practised as an advocate and is even said to have written much of the *Waverley Novels* while the dull court business droned on. A door to the far right of the building, labelled Court of Session, leads to the Great Hall which still retains a marvellous hammerbeam roof. Under this hall is the Laigh Parliament Hall which is a smaller hall once used by Oliver Cromwell as a stable.

Tucked into the wall of St Giles' opposite is a statue of John Knox, the Protestant reformer and the first minister of Edinburgh in the very church which he now stands by. Knox is buried under the tarmac which covers the old graveyard of the church. A narrow passage takes you through to West Parliament Square where on your left is the 19th century Signet Library belonging to the Society of Writers to Her Majesty's Signet which is a select group of solicitors.

We now come to the west end of Edinburgh's most famous church, St Giles' named after a Greek hermit of the 6th century. Save for St Margaret's Chapel in the Castle, this is the oldest church in the city although only 4 massive pillars remain from the original building erected around 1120. This church replaced an earlier 9th century church. Only really a Cathedral (i.e. the seat of a bishop) for five years in the 17th century, this is the High Kirk of Edinburgh, although rarely called by its proper title.

Most of the present building, including its distinctive crown spire, dates from the 15th century; the church having been burnt by the invading English in 1385. In its time St Giles' has been divided up into 4 separate churches and it was not until 1883 that it became one again. Before this in 1829 the church underwent rather drastic restoration by William Burn who put a smooth exterior onto the old rubble walls. In 1910 the Thistle Chapel designed by Sir Robert Lorimer was added to the east end.

Inside the Cathedral a plaque by a side chapel marks the spot where in 1637 the legendary, and possibly mythical, Jenny Geddes threw her stool at Dean Hannay as he read the new Liturgy which seemed to the congregation to smack of popery, and thus it is said she 'struck the first blow in the great struggle for freedom of conscience'.

Turning now with your back to the church, the quiet dignified scene is a far cry from the turbulent and chaotic picture which would have met your eyes up to the 19th century. For instance, the heart-shaped set of cobbles to the left of the church's doorway mark the site of the old Tolbooth. As its name indicates this was once a booth for collecting tolls. It also housed meetings of the Town Council and Scottish Parliament but it is best known as the prison described by Sir Water Scott in *The Heart of Midlothian*. The heads of executed criminals were placed for general view on its walls.

To add to our picture, imagine a row of high wooden-fronted tenements running parallel with St Giles'. These were the 'Luckenbooths' or locked booths with shops on the ground floor and the homes of merchants above. At points the road was only 15 feet wide, and to add to the bustle were the 'Krames', market stalls in a narrow passage by the church which sold cheaper goods including many toys. Lord Cockburn likened the 18th century scene to 'one of the

Arabian nights' bazaars in Baghdad'. In 1815 the Luckenbooths were demolished, followed by the Tolbooth in 1817. The door of the old Tolbooth was taken away by Sir Walter Scott to his home, Abbotsford, where it remains today.

Parliament Square is completed by the Regional Chambers which now house the headquarters of the Lothian Regional Council.

Just before you cross George IV Bridge, notice 3 brass plaques in the road which mark the last public execution in Edinburgh in 1864. Brodie's Close, now shut off, was named after the father of the infamous William Brodie. Said to be the original *Dr Jekyll and Mr Hyde*, he was an honoured craftsman and Deacon by day and a ruthless burglar by night. Brodie was finally caught and hanged in 1870.

Riddle's Close is worth a look for the unusual house of Bailie McMorran with an outside wooden stair. The unfortunate owner of this house was killed by a student in a riot over school holidays in 1595. In 1593 a great banquet was held in the close for James VI whilst David Hume lived here for a short while in the 18th century.

In a house off Upper Bow to the left, once lived the colourful and macabre Major Thomas Weir and his sister, Grizel. Like Deacon Brodie they preserved an air of devout respectability until Major Weir, reaching old age, confessed that he was a servant of the devil. Fantastic stories were told of his black staff going out alone to carry out his evil work and in 1670 Weir was sentenced to be strangled and burned. His sister, his partner in his Satanic crimes, was hanged in the Grassmarket.

Note the circle of cobble stones on the traffic island in the middle of Upper Bow which mark the site of the old Butter Tron where cheese and butter were weighed. Across the road we come to the tallest spire in Edinburgh, some 73 metres high, belonging to the Tolbooth Kirk. This was designed by two famous architects, James Gillespie Graham and Augustus Pugin, and originally housed the meetings of the Assembly of the Church of Scotland before Assembly Hall was built opposite.

As the Castle begins to come into view we pass Boswell Court where a plaque tells of a reputed meeting between Boswell and Johnson here in 1770. Walking by the Victorian Castlehill school we come finally to Cannonball House. You will have to walk around to the west wall facing the Castle to see why this house is so called, for lodged in this wall is an old cannonball. Thought by many to have been shot from the Castle in the Jacobite rising of 1745, in fact, less romantically, it marks the height to which the water from the city's first piped water supply could rise by gravitation.

We are now back at the Castle Esplanade – the end of this walk.

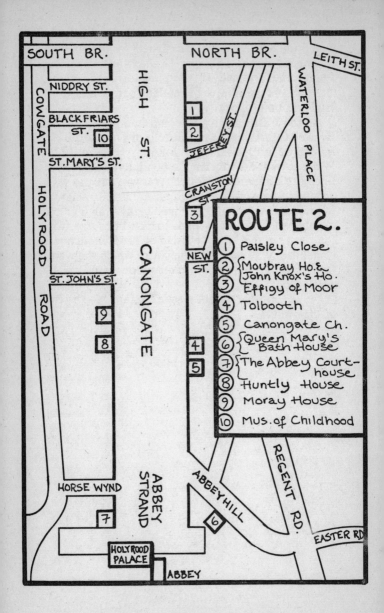

SOUTH BR. NORTH BR. LEITH ST.

NIDDRY ST.

COWGATE

BLACKFRIARS ST.

10

ST. MARY'S ST.

HIGH ST.

WATERLOO PLACE

JEFFERY ST.

1
2

CRANSTON ST.

3

HOLYROOD ROAD

ST. JOHN'S ST.

NEW ST.

CANONGATE

9

8

4

5

ROUTE 2.

① Paisley Close
② Moubray Ho. & John Knox's Ho.
③ Effigy of Moor
④ Tolbooth
⑤ Canongate Ch.
⑥ Queen Mary's Bath House
⑦ The Abbey Court-house
⑧ Huntly House
⑨ Moray House
⑩ Mus. of Childhood

REGENT RD.

HORSE WYND

ABBEY STRAND

ABBEY HILL

7

6

EASTER RD

HOLYROOD PALACE

ABBEY

Route 2

THE ROYAL MILE – PALACE END

Start this part of the walk down the Royal Mile at the North Bridge which was built at the turn of the century to replace the original 18th century bridge. Walking down towards the Palace on the left-hand side of the road, we come to Carruber Close where the poet Allan Ramsay once lived. In 1736 he opened a theatre in the close but it was soon closed by the disapproving authorities. In Bishop's Close next door, another poet Robert Burns, attended French lessons in the winter of 1786.

Above the entrance of Paisley Close, look up to see a boy's face carved in stone with an inscription above it, 'Heave awa' chaps, I'm no dead yet'. These words were supposed to have been shouted by a boy as rescuers cleared the debris away, after buildings on the site had collapsed in 1861. 35 people were not so lucky and died. Walk past the building of the Carruber Close Mission built in 1833, on past Monteith and Trunk's Close, until you come to the fine Moubray House. Built about 1462, although much altered in the 17th century, this is one of the oldest houses in the city. A plaque on the first floor wall commemorates the Scottish portrait painter, George Jameson, who lived here in the 1630s. It was also from here that Daniel Defoe edited the *Edinburgh Courant* in 1710.

Jutting out from Moubray House is one of the most famous houses in Edinburgh, the house of John Knox. Best seen from across the road, it has such distinctive features as overhanging upper wooden floors and crow-step gables, which were typical of mid-16th century architecture. Stories are told of Knox, the fiery Protestant reformer, haranguing the crowd from the house where he was thought to have lived from 1561–72. Now, however, it is beginning to seem doubtful that Knox lived here at all. But it was the house's association with Knox which saved it from destruction in 1849, whilst it is now a museum dedicated to Knox and the Scottish Reformation.

By contrast, we come next to the modern Netherbow Arts Centre, but since it is built in the style of an old Edinburgh town house it harmonises well with its surroundings. A model of the original Netherbow Port hangs above the entrance whilst, at the next crossroads, brass plaques in the road mark the site of the old Netherbow Port, one of the gates to the old city. With circular towers and a spire it must have formed an impressive entrance to the city, particularly as the heads of criminals were displayed on spikes above the gate!

We are now in the Canongate which until 1856 was a separate burgh from Edinburgh. It is so called because this area was the walk way or 'gait' of the canons of Holyrood Abbey. With the growth of Holyrood Palace after 1506, Canongate became a desirable residential quarter, close to the Court, and free from the overcrowding within the walled city of Edinburgh. Citizens used to commute between Edinburgh and Canongate by sedan chair.

Just beyond the entrance to Mid-Common Close, look up to see the carving of a Moor on the left of the building. This commemorates the romantic story of Andrew Gray who escaped to sea after being sentenced to death for leading a riot in the 17th century. After achieving fame in Morocco, he returned disguised as a Moor, to revenge himself on Edinburgh. However, he found the Lord Provost's daughter to be ill, cured her, and finding the girl to be his cousin married her, and set up home in a house named, 'Morocco Land', on this spot.

Notice the way this part of the Royal Mile has been greatly reconstructed. Much of this took place at the end of the 1950s and the restorers have managed to revive old styles of Edinburgh architecture at the same time as lightening the austerity of the Royal Mile through the colour-washed houses. Just after the Tolbooth clock comes into view, keep your eyes peeled for Bible Land, so named because of the sculptured Bible above the entrance, showing Psalm No. 133. This was built by the Incorporation of Cordiners (Shoemakers) who practised their craft here.

We now come to the Tolbooth built in 1591, which served as courthouse, prison and council-house for Canongate. The building contains many Latin inscriptions as well as the coat of arms of the Burgh of Canongate. But as you look at these, keep an eye on the traffic from Tolbooth Wynd, which is deceptively busy. The present clock is from 1820 whilst Tolbooth is now a city museum and brass-rubbing centre.

Set back from the road is the attractive Canongate Church with its unusual curved gables. This church, built in 1688, has a churchyard worthy of investigation. Many famous people are buried here, including the economist and author of the *Wealth of Nations*, Adam Smith, and Robert Burns' 'Clarinda', Mrs Agnes McLehose. Burns fell passionately in love with the lady and styling himself as, 'Sylvander' wrote romantic poetry to her as, 'Clarinda'. In one verse he wrote:

Had we never loved sae kindly,
Had we never lov'd sae blindly,
Never met or never parted,
We had ne'er been broken hearted.'

Robert Fergusson the poet, who is also buried here, was a great source of inspiration to Burns. At his grave is a headstone paid for by Burns with a dedication and a verse of Burns' poetry. The graveyard also contains the Canongate mercat cross which once stood on the street.

Little Lochend Close, another fine example of reconstruction, gives access to Panmure House, now a special school but once the house of Adam Smith from 1778 until his death in 1790. The pretty whitewashed Canongate Manse at Reid's Court was built in 1690 as a coaching inn.

Your walk is now increasingly likely to be permeated by the smell of beer from Holyrood Brewery down the road. This area has always been popular with brewers because of the excellent water of the local springs and the tax exemption which Canongate offered when it was still outside the city walls.

At Brown's Close is a plaque marking the site of Golfer's Land, built by a 17th century shoemaker, John Paterson. The house was built with the winnings from partnering the future James VII of Scotland, James II of Britain, in a match to defend Scottish golfing supremacy against the challenge of two English lords. Next door, and again now remembered only by a plaque, was Jenny Ha's Change House, a famous inn from 1600 to 1857 and run at one time by Jenny Hall, famous for her potent claret.

As Holyrood Palace begins to come into view we pass Whitefoord House, now a home for veteran servicemen, and come to the very attractive White Horse Close. Originally the Royal Mews in the 16th century, it was from here that the stagecoach left for London from the 17th century onwards. The close was restored and rebuilt in 1965. Just before the traffic island notice a circle of cobbles in the road which mark the site of the old Girth Cross, once the site of proclamations and executions.

Cross the road into the last part of the Royal Mile, the Abbey Strand, at whose head you will find 3 Ss in the road. These marked the beginning of sanctuary which was offered by the Abbey to debtors right up to 1880 when imprisonment for debt was abolished. Many of the debtors were aristocratic men and enjoyed a pleasant life in the Sanctuary which extended right over Holyrood Park. Nicknamed, 'Abbey Lairds', they lived in the Abbey Sanctuary Buildings to the left. These 16th century buildings are best seen from Abbeyhill to the left, where you will also find the curious building in the Palace's grounds, called Queen Mary's Bath House. This was probably not a bath house but a pavillion.

Returning to Abbey Strand we soon come to the fine wrought iron Palace gates which provide access to the Palace grounds. Although the name, 'Holyrood' is usually associated with the Palace, an abbey was actually the first building to be erected here, and part still remains. According to the legend, in 1128, David I, King of the Scots, went hunting on these lands, then on the edge of a great forest, and was charged by a stag which pinned him to the ground. Trying to grasp the stag's antlers he found the stag had vanished and in place of his horns was a crucifix. In gratitude for his escape the King built the Abbey of the Holy Rood or Cross. The Abbey thrived until the Revolution of 1688 when the Abbey Church was badly damaged.

The Palace, originally a guest house attached to the Abbey, was made into a Royal residence by King James IV in 1501. It was here that Mary, Queen of Scots lived and where her Italian secretary David Rizzio, was murdered. It is said that bloodstains, carefully repainted each year, used to mark the site of the murder, but now there is only a plaque on the spot. The Palace was greatly added to in the reign of Charles II with a new south-west tower (to the right), and in fact most of the Palace dates from this time. In the courtyard is a rather over-ornate Victorian fountain whilst the Palace enjoys a particularly fine backdrop of Salisbury Crags and Arthur's Seat.

At this point you may like to visit the Palace appartments where, apart from the rooms of Mary, Queen of Scots and the site of Rizzio's murder, you can also see the fine Picture Gallery. This contains one hundred and eleven portraits of Scottish monarchs, all of which were painted for Charles II between 1684–6 by a Dutch artist called Jakob de Wet of Haarlem. It was also here that another Charles, the Young Pretender Charles Stuart, held balls in his brief occupation of the Palace in 1745.

Leaving the Palace look at the Abbey Courthouse on the left which shows the outline of the old Gothic Porch and Gatehouse, demolished in 1753. The Scottish Court once sat in the Abbey Courthouse. On the corner of Horse Wynd, so called because it led to stables, the workshops were once the Victorian Holyrood Free Church of Scotland.

Crossing the road, the bottom of Canongate contains new and uninteresting buildings but the view further up the road is a harmonious one reflecting the success of the reconstruction work. The solid respectability of Queensberry House, now a hospital, belies the stories of cannabalism associated with the house. The story goes that the second Duke of Queensberry returned one day to find his eldest son had roasted a kitchen boy on a spit, and was now feasting on his flesh!

Walking past the entrance to Holyrood Brewery whose smell will either entice or repel, according to taste, we arrive at the Scottish Crafts Centre, situated in Acheson House. Go in through the gate to see this very attractive house built in 1633 for Sir Archibald Acheson of Glencairney. Just past Acheson House you can see the sign of the drummer and crier over

Huntly House. This is another fine house built in 1570 with projecting upper floors as in John Knox's house. On the front of the building you can see Latin plaques containing aphorisms such as, 'Today for me, tomorrow for thee, why therefore carest thou?' and 'I am old but renew my youth'. These have given the building the nickname of the 'Speaking House'. Huntly House is now a museum of local history and amongst its many exhibits is the 1638 National Covenant, protesting against attempts to introduce episcopacy to Scotland. The entrance to Huntly House is through Bakehouse Close while next door, Sugar House Close once led to a sugar refinery.

In order to appreciate the grandeur of Moray House, cross the road and look up to the windows above the balcony where you can glimpse the fine plastered ceilings. This house was built in 1628 and once had beautiful gardens favoured by Oliver Cromwell. Alas these gardens are now gone and the house is part of a teacher training college. In the grounds is a 17th century summer house where it is believed the Treaty of the Act of Union with England in 1707 received some signatures.

Turn left into St John's Street which contains a couple of interesting buildings on the right. The Masonic Canongate Kilwinning Lodge built in 1736, is thought to be the oldest Masonic lodge-room in the world, and it once gave Robert Burns the title of the lodge's poet laureate. Further down is the Priory of the old Order of the Knights of St John.

Back on the Royal Mile again, the Canongate Theatre was built in 1746 in the Old Playhouse Close, but it led a rowdy life and finally the seats and fittings were torn up for ammunition, before the theatre was closed in 1767. Chessel Court which was the scene of the undoing of Deacon Brodie's night robberies (see page 18), is now a beautifully restored colour-washed development. The modern block fronting onto the Canongate is a replica of the original building which was erected here in 1769. In the courtyard itself the buildings ahead of you and to the right (i.e. south and east blocks) are restored 18th century buildings, and it was in one of these that Deacon Brodie was caught red-handed in 1788.

Once you arrive at World End's Close you are back within the original city of Edinburgh. A little parochially, this close was so called as the last close before the Flodden Wall and the end of Edinburgh. Tweeddale, at the back of Tweeddale Court, was once the Head Office of the British Linen Bank and then became the offices of the publisher, Oliver & Boyd. The original wrought iron gates can still be seen whilst to the right is the 18th century shed for sedan chairs. A gaily coloured sign marks the Museum of Childhood, established in 1955, as the first museum in the world devoted purely to the history of childhood. It contains dolls, puppets, displays of toys, etc., fascinating to adults and children alike.

South Gray's Close once contained the Royal Mint while a little further down, Blackfriars Street formerly led to the monastery of the black or Dominican friars on the Cowgate below. Cross Niddry Street to return to the South Bridge, built 1785–6, and the end of the walk, unless you are combining walks, in which case turn to page 31 and walk back up to the Castle.

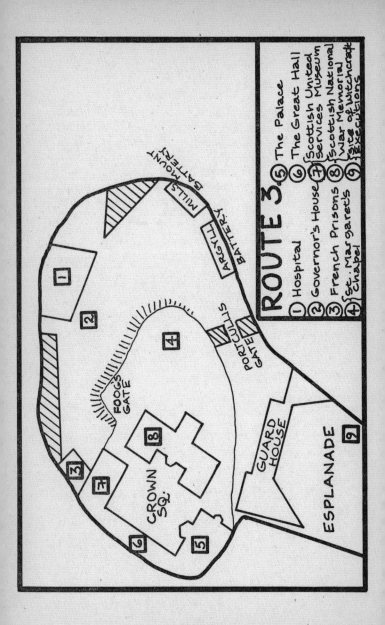

ROUTE 3

1. Hospital
2. Governor's House
3. French Prisons
4. St. Margaret's Chapel
5. The Palace
6. The Great Hall
7. Scottish United Services Museum
8. Scottish National War Memorial
9. Site of Witchcraft Executions

MILLS MOUNT BATTERY

ARGYLL BATTERY

PORTCULLIS GATE

FOOG'S GATE

CROWN SQ.

GUARD HOUSE

ESPLANADE

Route 3

THE CASTLE

This is a brief walk around Edinburgh Castle which you may like to do before or after some of the other routes – for instance the walk down the Royal Mile (see page 11), or to the Grassmarket (see page 37), which both start from the Castle Esplanade.

Much of the fascination of the Castle lies in its position high above the city, standing on a crop of rock from an extinct volcano. In the Ice Age the north and south sides were formed into steep banks making it a marvellous defensive site. There has been some form of fortress on this rock from the 11th century onwards although it is thought that there was some occupation here as early as the 6th century. Throughout mediaeval times the Castle has acted as an impressive fortress with more defences being added as necessary.

Unlike most castles in Britain, Edinburgh Castle continued to adapt to military requirements until the 19th century and even now it is a very functional building which houses regimental headquarters. This means, however, that much of the Castle is relatively new and therefore can be disappointing to those more accustomed to the grandeur of mediaeval fortresses. But the Castle is still well worth a visit particularly as it gives you some superb views of Edinburgh.

Begin your walk in the Castle Esplanade which has now been made world famous by the Edinburgh Military Tatoo which takes place here at Festival time. Originally formed by glacial action, nature's work was aided in the 18th and 19th centuries when a parade ground was formed. Looking out from the left-hand side of the Esplanade you have a fine panorama over the city. Directly below is the Grass-market whilst in the centre of the picture is the magnificent Jacobean Heriot's Hospital. Further in the distance are the Pentland Hills.

As you walk towards the Castle drawbridge you may be surprised to know that you are treading on a fraction of Nova Scotian soil. This came about in the 17th century when baronetcies were offered for sale in the colony to encourage settlement there and make money for the Crown. Before these were legal the new baronets had to take 'saisin' which involved accepting a tiny part of the soil of the new territory, in this case Nova Scotia. This custom posed all sorts of practical problems given the dangers and distances involved in travelling to the colony. These problems were solved by passing a piece of legal fiction naming parts of the Esplanade Nova Scotian soil so 'saisin' could be carried out on the home soil. In 1953 the Prime Minister of Nova Scotia came to Edinburgh and sprinkled some of his country's earth on the Esplanade, as a confirmation of this curious state of affairs.

Walk over the drawbridge which was built in 1887 as the last retractable drawbridge in Scotland. To either side are statues of two Scottish heroes. On the left is Robert the Bruce, victor of the Battle of Bannockburn in 1314 and on the right, Sir William Wallace who eventually perished in 1305 at the hands of King Edward I of England.

Once through the entrance it is possible to see the curves of the Half-Moon Battery. Built as part of the Castle's defences in the 1570s, it surrounds the remains of a tower built by David II in the 14th century. Follow the road through another gateway, the Portcullis Gate, part of which was also built in the 1570s. This brings you up onto the Argyll Battery with its six enormous guns trained onto the city. The views from here are wonderful with the Town spread out in the centre while to the right the monuments of Calton Hill can be seen against a backcloth of the sea.

Round to the right is Mill's Mount Battery from where the one o'clock gun is fired. This can give the unsuspecting visitor a great shock particularly if he happens to be standing right by the canon at the fatal hour. Bearing round to the left you come to the most domestic part of the Castle. On the right is the Governor's house which was built in 1742 and is now used as an Officer's Mess. Behind this are the New Barracks, built in the 1790s, which at 6 storeys high are the tallest buildings in the Castle.

To the right of this down a small path is the hospital. Mainly built in 1748, the building was embellished and altered to form a hospital in the 1890s. To the left of these buildings are the French Prisons which were originally built in order to provide a flat roof for the Great Hall above. Their name, however, comes from the time in the late 18th, early 19th centuries when they housed French prisoners of war who have left their mark in the form of carvings on the wall.

The French Prisons house Edinburgh's most famous canon, Mons Meg. This dates from the 1440s and was used up to 1681 when it burst during firing. Later it was sent off to the Tower of London and it was only Sir Water Scott's influence which led to its eventual return in Edinburgh in 1829. It is hoped to create an artillery museum here.

The road sweeps out through Foog's Gate on its way to Crown Square. But before you reach the square notice St Margaret's Chapel, the small building to the left. Here also used to stand Mons Meg until it was moved to a more sheltered home.

St Margaret's Chapel is the oldest building not only in the Castle but also in the whole of Edinburgh.

Probably built at the beginning of the 12th century, it was dedicated to the saintly Queen Margaret, the wife of King Malcolm III who was responsible for establishing the nucleus of a permanent fortress on the Castle rock. Queen Margaret herself is said to have died of grief when she was told of her husband and son's deaths in 1093. For a long time in secular use, its real nature was rediscovered in 1846. Go into the chapel which is a simple building distinguished by the attractive arch in the middle, decorated with a zig-zig pattern, and the vaulted apse which contains the altar.

Bearing round to the right you come out into Crown Square which as the mediaeval heart of the Castle is perhaps the most interesting part. The left-hand side of the square is dominated by the palace with its curious elongated tower. Mainly built in the early 16th century, it was here that the future King of Scotland and England, James VI and I, was born to Mary, Queen of Scots. It is well worth following the signs to the Crown Room where the Scottish Crown, Sword and Sceptre are beautifully displayed under a wooden vaulted roof. When Scotland united with England in 1707 the Royal regalia were walled up for protection only to appear again in the 19th century. At right angles to the Palace is the Great Hall which has a magnificent timber roof and a fine display of arms. Formerly divided up into four floors and used as a hospital the hall was restored to one building at the end of the 19th century.

Walking round the square we come to the Scottish National War Memorial which was built in 1927 by Sir Robert Lorimer. This has a richly decorated interior and a visit there is a solemn and moving experience. Each regiment has its own separate memorial and Book of Honour but the climax of the memorial is the casket given by George V and Queen Mary which contains the names of 100,000 Scots who died in the First World War. The square is completed by the Scottish United Services Museum.

Walking back towards St Margaret's Chapel go down the Lang Steps to the Portcullis Gate. Notice the plaque on the wall which recalls the heroic feat of the Earl of Moray in 1313 when, together with a band of armed men, he climbed the Castle wall and rescued it from the English.

Leaving the Castle you pass by several memorials and statues on the left including those to Ensign Ewart and Earl Haig. Ewart achieved fame at the Battle of Waterloo when he stole the ensign of one of the French Regiments. Bearing an eagle, this ensign then became the basis of the eagle badge of the Royal Scots Greys. Beyond this is the equestrian statue of Earl Haig and horse-lovers may be able to spot the odd pose of the horse which is said to be anatomically impossible.

Right at the end of the Esplanade is a bronze plaque marking the spot where 300 unfortunate women suspected of being witches were burnt to death between 1479–1722. If you look closely at the plaque you can see two female faces, one obviously good, the other evil. This was a piece of deliberate symbolism designed to show that some women were pure and presumably died unjustly but that others were truly evil and thus we are left to assume got their just deserts. A modern interpretation of the terrible fate of these women might read somewhat differently!

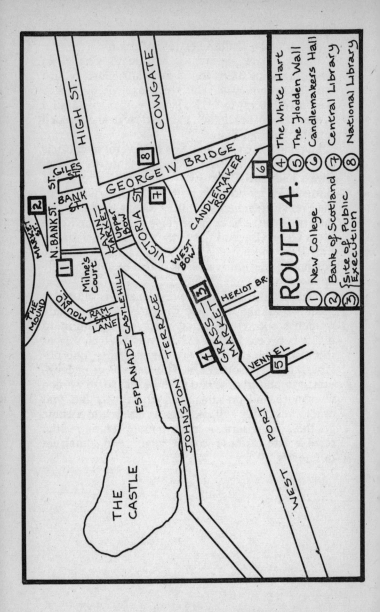

ROUTE 4.

① New College
② Bank of Scotland
③ Site of Public Execution
④ The White Hart
⑤ The Flodden Wall
⑥ Candlemakers Hall
⑦ Central Library
⑧ National Library

Route 4

THE GRASSMARKET
AND SURROUNDING AREA

The Grassmarket is one of the most distinctive parts of the Old Town and like the Royal Mile has many stories, some quite gruesome, to tell.

Start your walk at the top of Castle Hill at the Castle Esplanade. It is possible to walk down the steps in Castle Wynd, to your right, straight into the Grassmarket. However, this walk takes you a longer way round in order to see more of the Old Town.

Turn left down Ramsay Lane and pass by the attractive and unusual Ramsay Garden. This is a colourful collection of buildings with tall towers and crow-stepped gables, containing Ramsay Lodge, nicknamed 'Goose Pie' because of its curious shape, and the one-time home of the poet Allan Ramsay. The lane gives you marvellous views over Princes Street and the art galleries at the bottom of the Mound while behind these, gaps in the buildings provide glimpses of the sea and hills of Fife.

Following the road round to the right we come to the twin towers of New College. This was built by William Playfair, the same architect of the galleries below, but in a different and slightly less successful style. The College was built for the new Free Church in 1846–50 after it had split off from the Church of Scotland in the 'Disruption' of 1843. It is now the Faculty of Divinity for the University and, if you walk inside the courtyard, you will find a statue of the great Protestant reformer, John Knox. The Assembly Hall for the Church of Scotland is at the top of the courtyard.

Returning to the street you can see the grand domed headquarters of the Bank of Scotland which we will see more clearly at the end of the walk. Notice its commanding position above the New Town and in fact the Bank is often the first sight which the traveller, newly arrived at Waverley Station, sees as he walks up to Waverley Bridge and looks up to the ridge of the Old Town. It is a particularly magnificent sight at night when the bank is floodlit.

Turn right just pass New College and walk up the stairs leading to Milne's Court. This is a 17th century courtyard which was reconstructed in 1971 and is now used as University halls of residence. Leaving the court cross the Lawnmarket and go straight down the steep slope of Upper Bow.

This used to be the main route up to the Royal Mile. The road ran up from the Grassmarket as the West Bow which then became the Upper Bow as it neared the top. You can roughly follow the original route and appreciate quite how steep this street was. To do this descend the steps at the end of the short street which brings you to Victoria Street at the top of West Bow. You can now understand the necessity, perceived in the 19th century, for changing the line of the street and creating Victoria Street along with George IV Bridge to provide a more manageable entry to the Lawnmarket.

Turn right and follow the road as it becomes West Bow and begins to bend round to the left. The street contains some fascinating late 17th, early 18th century buildings. Cross over to the left to see some of the most interesting houses on the right such as No. 89, a tall stone building with crow-stepped gables. Next door to this, No. 93 has two round holes just under the roof, for pigeons to go in and out. Look at the house on the corner which has an old built up doorway and is inscribed, '16 Blessed Be God For Al His

Giftis 66'. It is thought that this house was possibly built in the 15th century and reconstructed in 1666.

In the centre of the road is the old Bowfoot Well. Before the days of piped water to houses this well was one of many which provided a vital form of water supply. Those who could afford it paid carriers or 'caddies' (as on golf-courses) to bring the water to them in their houses around the Royal Mile; the poorer people had to climb up and down the steep slope themselves. It is now an ornate construction, first erected in 1671 but greatly altered and embellished by the Victorians in 1861, who made it into a drinking fountain.

Turn right and you are now in the Grassmarket, which was laid out in the 16th century in the same rectangular shape as you find today. Close to the Castle and to the Cowgate to the East (formerly the site of Greyfriars Monastery and then the home of wealthy citizens), the Grassmarket became the chief agricultural market of the city. A weekly market was still being held here as late as 1911. Now, by contrast, the Grassmarket is lined by expensive and exclusive shops.

The Grassmarket also had a less benign face for it was a place of public execution. The most famous people to die here were the Covenanters who are remembered by a St Andrew's Cross in the middle of the road which is now fenced off. Following the signing of the National Covenant in 1638 protesting their belief in the Presbyterian form of Church Government, hundreds were persecuted, killed or outlawed, until the remnants were imprisoned in the open and freezing prison in the Greyfriars Churchyard (see page 135). Many of those who survived that ordeal were hanged in the Grassmarket, leading to the phrase, 'Let him glorify God in the Grassmarket.' The inscription round the cross is to the effect that,

'On this spot many martyrs and Covenanters died for the Protestant Faith.' The words are formed in a circle and so it is not clear quite where the sentence begins and ends.

The site remained the place for public executions until 1784 during which time many famous Edinburgh criminals met their death here, including the Jekyll and Hyde character, Deacon Brodie. One person who miraculously faced the rope and lived to tell the tale was 'Half-Hangit Maggie' who was hanged in the Grassmarket in 1724 for the murder of her young baby. While being taken back to her home in Musselburgh by friends, the 'corspe' sat up from her coffin, and subsequently lived to have more children and become an ale-house keeper in the city.

Nearby in an old close another execution took place, although this time at the hands of the mob. In 1746 after the execution of a popular hero, the onlookers rioted and threw stones at John Porteous, the arrogant and hated Captain of the Town Guard. Porteous ordered the crowd to be fired on, so killing 9 people. He was subsequently condemned to death but was granted a reprieve by Queen Caroline, acting for George II. The crowd, enraged by this, broke into the Tolbooth prison and hung Porteous from a dyer's pole. A story is told that the rope was bought for a shilling from a nearby shopkeeper who then screwed the coin, now blood money, onto his counter where it remained for many years. The Porteous incident, reflecting the Scottish resentment of the English throne, is immortalised in Scott's *The Heart of Midlothian*.

Walking down the right side of the Grassmarket you pass the pub aptly named, the Last Drop. Notice the inscription over the door in the middle of the pub. This reads the same as that on the house at the corner with West Bow while the faint initials which you can just see belonged to James Lightbodie and his wife Geillis, who originally owned the house.

Further on, the White Hart is an old coaching inn from the 18th century and was frequented by many famous literary figures including Robert Burns and William Wordsworth.

A couple of doors down, the Beehive Inn formerly provided lodgings for the carriers who delivered the goods bought and sold in the Grassmarket. It was in these sorts of establishments that the notorious murderers, Burke and Hare, hunted for their victims. Their dastardly crimes first began when one of the tenants of Hare, who kept a lodging house, died. The body was sold to the anatomist, John Knox, who was in need of bodies for dissecting purposes and was prepared to pay handsomely for them. Spurred on by this source of easy cash the two friends began to 'create' their own corpses by offering cheap food and lodgings to the poor and friendless, and then suffocating them. At least 16, possibly as many as 30, died before their crimes were detected. Hare turned King's evidence and so it was only Burke that hanged for his crimes.

Right at the end of the row, in the shadow of the Castle, is the old Greyfriars Mission Building dating from the 19th century, with an antique shop below. The narrow part of the Grassmarket's rectangle contains old carriers' quarters above which is the inscription, 'Let Glasgow Flourish' – a very odd sentiment to be seen in a town which is hardly renowned for its friendly feelings towards Glasgow!

At the end of the row was once the west gate in the Flodden Wall and the entrance to the city; and the name of the street, West Port, is a reminder of this. The gate was knocked down in the 19th century to help the flow of traffic. At the top of the West Port, but now demolished, was Tanner's Close which contained the lodging house that the hapless victims of Burke and Hare were enticed to.

The Flodden Wall was hastily erected to defend the city from possible siege after the Scots were dramatically beaten by the English at the Battle of Flodden in 1513. Remnants of it still remain and, if you cross West Port onto the long side of the Grassmarket and turn up right into the Vennel, you can see the best preserved part. About half-way up the path, the wall begins with a small tower-like projection and continues up on the left-hand side. Before it fell into ruins the wall came down from the Half-Moon Battery of the Castle and across the Grassmarket and up the Vennel, and then went on to encircle the south side of the city.

Retrace your steps to the Grassmarket which is dominated on this side by two modern buildings. The stark architecture of the first of these, the Mountbatten Building, part of Heriot Watt University, is ill-fitted to its surroundings. Moreover it replaced the handsome classically-styled building of the Cornmarket which not only housed the business side of the market but also hosted banquets and political meetings at which Gladstone once spoke.

To the right, Heriot Bridge once led to the main entrance of the George Heriot School or Hospital, whose towers are just visible. In the 19th century the entry was moved to Lauriston Place on the other side of the school. The other modern building, Uberior House, belonging to the Bank of Scotland, is slightly more successful in harmonising with the rest of the Grassmarket.

The rest of this side is taken up by the Castle Trades Hostel. This is only one of the hostels still operating in the Grassmarket, with the Greyfriars Mission opposite and the Salvation Army Hostel at the corner of West Port, which make a stark contrast with the opulence of the Grassmarket shops. The foundation of these hostels lies in the old carrier lodgings when the men carrying the goods needed somewhere cheap to stay.

Before you leave the Grassmarket notice the sign to the Traverse Theatre to the left which provides and stimulates experimental theatre in Edinburgh.

Turn right into the Cowgate. This road gets its name from the days when it was the route taken by the cows between grazing lands, for gate or gait means walkway. Once a highly desirable residential area with aristocratic houses, it has declined dramatically and is now just a busy traffic route running under George IV and South Bridges. Therefore instead of continuing on this road, turn right into Candlemaker Row.

This street derives its quaint name from the candlemakers who set up shop here after they were banned from the Old Town in 1654. Candlemaking was always a rather unsociable activity because of the smell and danger of melting tallow and when one of the workshops caught fire the candlemakers were finally forced out beyond the city walls to this spot. In the early 18th century they built better houses some of which remain at the top of the street. The house at the top was the old convening hall and dates above the door refer to the erection and subsequent restoration of the building.

Candlemaker Row brings you out by the fountain of Greyfriars Bobby, the famous dog who earned the freedom of the city by keeping faithful watch over his master's grave for 14 years. Behind this is Greyfriars Churchyard which you may wish to explore (see page 134). Turn left into George IV Bridge, built in 1834 as a flat route out of the Old Town to George Square and the south beyond. Except when breaks in the buildings give glimpses of the Cowgate below you are not aware you are on a bridge. George IV Bridge is dominated by two large libraries.

On the left is the Central Library built in 1890 from a bequest by Andrew Carnegie for the building of a public library in the city. A bust of the library's benefactor stands in the hallway above the stairs. The library contains a fine collection on local and Scottish history, as well as a Fine Art Library. Its exterior is in an elaborate French style, contrasting with the massive National Library opposite.

The largest library in Scotland, the National Library has a symmetrical and relatively plain facade enlivened by statues representing the arts and sciences. Founded in 1956 from a core of books from the Advocates Library, it is a copyright library, entitled to receive a free copy of every book published under copyright in Britain.

As you near the junction with the Lawnmarket you pass by the Regional and County Offices on either side. You also have a fine view of the Bank of Scotland at the end of Bank Street ahead. The Bank of Scotland was founded in 1695 and for over a hundred years it had its offices in Bank Close in the Royal Mile. In 1802 it moved to its present site which was considered to be well placed between the New and Old Towns. In 1860 the original design was greatly altered and made more ornate by the architect David Bryce. The building is in an Italian style with a central green dome and turrets and smaller octagonal domes to the sides.

From the crossroads it is but a short walk to North Bridge where, if you choose, you can begin the walk down the Royal Mile to Holyrood Palace (see page 21).

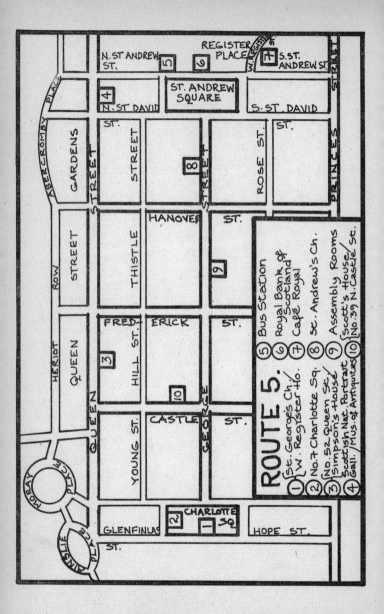

REGISTER PLACE

N. ST ANDREW ST.

⑤ ⑥ W. REGISTER ST. ⑦ S. ST. ANDREW ST.

④ N. ST DAVID

ST. ANDREW SQUARE

S. ST. DAVID

ABERCROMBY PLACE

GARDENS STREET

ST. STREET

⑧ STREET

ROSE ST. ST.

PRINCES STREET

ROW

STREET

THISTLE STREET

HANOVER ST.

ST.

⑨

Bus Station

Royal Bank of Scotland

Cape Royal

St. Andrew's Ch.

Assembly Rooms

Scott's House

No. 39 N. Castle St.

HERIOT

QUEEN STREET

③

FRED-ERICK ST.

HILL ST.

ST.

⑩

⑤ ⑥ ⑦ ⑧ ⑨ ⑩

ROUTE 5.

St. George's Ch.

W. Register Ho.

No. 7 Charlotte Sq.

No. 52 Queen St. Simpson's House

Scottish Nat. Portrait Gall. / Mus. of Antiquites

① ② ③ ④

MORAY PLACE

QUEEN

YOUNG ST.

CASTLE ST.

GEORGE ST.

AINSLIE PLACE

GLENFINLAS ST.

② CHARLOTTE SQ

HOPE ST.

46

Route 5

THE FIRST NEW TOWN

> I charge you not to think of settling in London till you have first seen our New Town which exceeds anything you have seen in any part of the world. (David Hume to a friend in 1771.)

The New Town, not so new now of course, is the biggest Georgian development in Britain, and in this walk we can see only a portion of it. The part we shall be walking through was the first section to be built and is often referred to as the 'First New Town'.

This development was the conception of a young architect James Craig, the winner of the competition held in 1776 for a master plan for a new town. The Old Town around the Royal Mile had been getting more and more crowded, and the situation had finally become unbearable when a period of stability and peace led the population to increase yet further. It was time for Edinburgh to spread itself on to the lands beyond the Nor' Loch, which was now to be drained. It is these lands which we will be walking on, designed as a residential development, now the commercial and professional centre of Edinburgh.

As we walk round we will see that Craig's plan was a simple one – a grid iron pattern closed at each end by a square which were joined by a central street, George Street, and bounded on either side by 2 terraces, Princes and Queen Streets. In between these roads but parallel to them were the lesser streets, Rose and Thistle Streets, intended for 'shopkeepers and others', who were to serve the greater folk in the other streets.

Our walk begins in one of the two squares, Charlotte Square. This is easily the most elegant and gracious square in Edinburgh although its qualities can best be appreciated on a Sunday, when the race-track of cars has quietened down. If you stand with your back to St George's Church (West Register House) and look across to the north and south sides of the square, you can see that all the houses are not separate blocks but are deliberately designed to form one unit. Because their facade looks rather like a palace, this style of architecture is called, a 'Palace-front' style. The arch practitioner of this style was Robert Adam who provided the design for the entire square although, since he died in 1792 before the building of most of the square had been begun, only the north side, erected first, is completely faithful to Adam's original plans.

Robert Adam also provided a design for St George's Church, now West Register House, behind you. Probably because of financial reasons, Adam's plan was replaced with one by Robert Reid, the King's Architect. The substitution was the source of much ill-feeling at the time, the *Scots Magazine* reported that 'each part appears to have been designed with the same cool and deliberate bad taste which characterises the whole plan.' Over-harsh perhaps, but it is true that the church is too heavy and out of proportion with the square, even though its green dome, modelled on St Paul's, makes a fine sight in this part of the New Town.

With the equestrian statue of Prince Albert, unveiled by Queen Victoria in 1876, to the right of you in the gardens, walk round the square in a clockwise direction. As you walk, you pass the former homes of Edinburgh dignitaries such as Sir William Fettes at No. 13 and Lord Cockburn at No. 14.

At the end of the west side cross the road to the gardens side of the north row and notice the peculiarities of the 'Palace-front' style. There is a central colonnaded unit enriched by carvings, this is flanked by plainer houses until you reach the wings or ends of the row which are set slightly forward and decorated with flat pilasters.

Cross the road to examine the houses in detail and notice the fine wrought iron lamp stands with the curious horn-like structures half-way down. These, called 'link-horns', were used to extinguish the torch, and in varying designs crop up again throughout the New Town. It is said that Charlotte Square was once known as Edinburgh's Harley Street because of the number of doctors who lived there. Nowadays the main occupants are solicitors' firms and finance houses, but as a reminder of its former days, notice No. 9 where Professor Lister, famous for his work in antiseptic surgery, stayed from 1870–1877.

No. 7 Charlotte Square is now open to the public as a typical Georgian house. It is well worth a visit, the house, lovingly decorated and furnished, fully recaptures the sheer elegance which characterised the Georgians in their daily lives. The house also shows a short film on the history of the New Town. No. 6, the focal point of the row and the grandest of the houses, is the official residence of the Secretary of State for Scotland. Next door to this is the headquarters of the National Trust for Scotland.

The east side of the square is divided up by the entrance to George Street, the centre of the First New Town, but our route takes us left, down North Charlotte Street, at right angles to the north side of the square. With a magnificent view over later developments in the New Town and across the Forth to Fife, this road takes us down to Queen Street. This is the northern boundary of Craig's plan and, like Princes Street the southern boundary, it only has houses on one side of the road, (except for the first few yards). With its rather austere architecture and open aspect, this street can seem a little bleak at times, particularly when the famous Edinburgh winds are blowing!

Turn right into Queen Street and the buildings opposite soon give way to gardens, formally laid out in 1823, to which only residents have access. Several houses have fine ironwork, as, for instance, at No. 63, whilst Nos. 62 and 53 have literary associations. At the first lived Lord Jeffrey who was involved with the *Edinburgh Review*, whilst the second provided a home for a time for John Wilson, better known as 'Christopher North' of *Blackwoods Magazine*.

No. 52 next door housed the most famous resident of Queen Street, for it was here that Sir James Simpson first proved the anaesthetic powers of chloroform in 1847. His experiment was conclusive in no uncertain manner: Dr Simpson notes how, before sitting down to supper, he and his assistants, 'inhaled the fluid and were all under the mahogany in a trice, to my wife's consternation and alarm'.

Turn right into Frederick Street and walk up the hill a little way and turn first left into Thistle Street. The atmosphere and architecture of this narrow street is a complete contrast to the grand formality of Queen Street, although these smaller streets were an integral part of the New Town. An attractive road, it is full of small individual shops. Notice the lanes going off to the right and left, a pattern which is common throughout the First New Town. At the end of the street turn left into Hanover Street and right back into Queen Street.

Continue along the road and notice the way the ornate Nos. 9 and 10, built in 1845, contrast with the quiet elegance of No. 8, built by Robert Adam in 1770 and now forming part of the Royal College of Physicians. As the gardens opposite end, this side of the road is dominated by the Gothic building erected in 1890 by Rowand Anderson, to house the Scottish

National Portrait Gallery and the Museum of Antiquities. Together these house a magnificent collection, including the Roman Traprain Treasure, John Knox's pulpit, and in the Gallery, portraits from the early Stuart kings onwards. Outside, the statues in the walls are by Birnie Rhind. The chief funds for the museums came from an unknown benefactor, later revealed as J. R. Findlay, proprietor of *The Scotsman*.

From the museum retrace your steps slightly and turn up North St David Street into St Andrew Square. This was designed to match Charlotte Square but, unfortunately, it comes a poor second to the elegance of the former. Like its sister, however, it contains fine gardens, this time surrounding a figure of Lord Melville by Robert Forrest. Lord Melville stands high above the square on a Doric column 136 feet high by Sir William Burn. The residents were so concerned at the height of the column when it was being erected that they called in the engineer Robert Stevenson to advise on foundations.

St Andrew Square has been called the richest square in Britain and it certainly contains an astonishingly high proportion of banks and insurance companies. Walk round the square in a clockwise direction starting from the north side which is the best preserved part of the square. It begins with No. 21 where Henry Brougham who gave his name to a type of carriage was born in 1778, three years after the house was built. Nos. 22, 24 and 25 were also built in the 1770s and have been little altered although their line is broken by No. 23.

Unfortunately, facing you as you near the end of this row is the uninspiring bus station; more pleasing, although still new, is the Norwich Union Building. But more interesting is No. 35 built in 1769, which, as the Douglas Hotel in the 19th century, was patronised by Queen Victoria, Empress Eugenie and also

Sir Walter Scott who stayed there on his last visit to Edinburgh in 1832. Next door to this, set back behind ornate gates, is the most impressive building in the square. Now the Royal Bank of Scotland, this was once the house of Sir Lawrence Dundas, built in 1772–4 and designed by Sir William Chambers. This site was originally earmarked for St Andrew's Church which was intended to face St George's Church along George Street in Charlotte Square, but Sir Lawrence refused to yield his land, so the church had to be built in George Street itself. This selfishness can perhaps be forgiven for the resulting building is a superb Georgian house with balustrades and fine tracery under the roof. In front is a statue of the Earl of Hopetoun erected in 1834.

Turn left down into West Register Street and walk along a little way until you come to the Café Royal. Although the chief splendours of this Victorian building (built 1862) are inside, with Doulton Delft tile panels and stained glass windows, its facade, in the style of the Second Empire, suggests its individualistic flavour. Follow the road to the right onto Princes Street.

Turn right and walk down a little to see the way in which Princes Street, like Queen Street, is devoid of buildings on the left hand side. Then take the second right, South St David Street. On the right-hand side, just before you reach the square is a plaque recording the site of the home of David Hume who wrote *My Own Life* there, and died in the house in 1776. According to tradition, the inscription 'St David's Street' was chalked on the wall outside his house by a friend, presumably as an ironic joke at the expense of Hume's atheism.

Enter the square and turn left into George Street. This broad, straight road, 115 feet wide, was originally intended to link, symbolically as well as physically, the two squares. Charlotte Square was initially called St George's Square and so George Street, symbolising the monarch links the patron saints of England and Scotland, so reflecting the Union between the two countries in 1707. The street retains many Georgian houses even though some have had shop fronts added, and there are also some fine Victorian commercial buildings.

Immediately you enter the street you can see examples of the latter. Look to your right at the office of the Standard Life Assurance Company with sculptured figures above the door, illustrating the parable of the 10 virgins. To your left is the massive classical building of the Royal Bank of Scotland with its huge portico of 6 columns.

Facing the bank is St Andrew's Church, a curious, tall, thin building, built in 1875 by Major Frazer as the first church in the New Town. This church was the scene of the 'Disruption' in 1845, when 470 ministers walked out of the General Assembly of the Church of Scotland and formed their own Free Church of Scotland. They were protesting at the appointment of ministers by patronage and the Kirk's acquiescence in this outrage. The spire of the church is 168 feet high and was added later by William Sibbald in 1789.

At the corner of Hanover Street is a statue of George IV to commemorate his visit to Scotland in 1822. From here you have a fine open view across the Forth to the hills of Fife, and here you can see one of the great merits of Craig's plan for the New Town. Clever use was made of the superb natural position to give magnificent views which take you unawares at the intersections of roads. Cross Hanover Street and on the left is the impressive Bank c´ Scotland building, designed by David Bryce in 1874, once the head office of the Union Bank of Scotland when it was in existence. Ionic columns dominate its frontage while next door is the Royal Society whose past members include Robert Louis Stevenson and the German writer Goethe.

No. 52 George Street provided another home for James Simpson of chloroform fame whilst No. 60 provided refuge for Percy Shelley and his 16 year old sweetheart, Harriet Westbrook, when they eloped from England. Too young to marry under English law they were married by a Scottish parson. A few years later, Shelley and his wife again found refuge in Edinburgh, this time at 36 Frederick Street, when they were escaping from creditors.

This side of the road is dominated by the Assembly Rooms and Music Hall behind. This building, a little dour in appearance, was once the glittering centre of the aristocratic dancing assemblies in the New Town. It was also the scene of Scott's dramatic announcement in 1827, that he was indeed author of the *Waverley Novels,* a fact until then he had refused to admit. When the Edinburgh Assembly Rooms were opened in 1787, only the Rooms at Bath were bigger. The huge ball room, 92 feet long, is still in use.

No. 84, easily distinguished by the flashing lighthouse as the office of the Commissioners of Northern Lighthouses, is one of the few unspoilt Georgian buildings in the street. Across the road, No. 75 was the home for a while of Sir Walter Scott whilst if you go right, down North Castle Street, you will find No. 39 where Scott lived between 1800–1826, writing many of the *Waverley Novels* there. The house is one of a set of three which were reputedly designed by Robert Adam.

Return to George Street and the statue at the junction is of Thomas Chalmers who led the 'Disruption'. Further down notice Nos. 110 and 112 on the left and No. 125 on the right which are original Georgian houses. A few houses down at No. 133 is the stretch of pavement which was once nicknamed 'Giant's Causeway'. The author of this tag was Mr John Sinclair, compiler of the first *Statistical Account of Scotland* (as a precursor of the modern census) on account of the size of his 13 children, all of whom were over 6 feet tall. The house next door, No. 131, was used as an office by the architect William Burn from 1822 and by another architect David Bryce after 1844.

The trees and gracious lines of Charlotte Square with the green dome in the centre should be well in view by now, and so noticing the reconstructed facade of Nos. 127–9 (First Chicago National Bank) and the ornate Italian appearance of the Church of Scotland offices, leave George Street and return to Charlotte Square, the end of the walk.

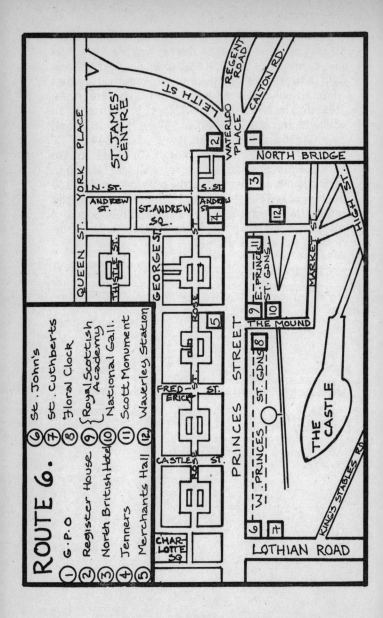

ROUTE 6.

① G.P.O
② Register House
③ North British Hotel
④ National Gall.
⑤ Waverley Station

⑥ St. John's
⑦ St. Cuthberts
⑧ Floral Clock
⑨ Royal Scottish Academy
⑩ National Gall.
⑪ Scott Monument
⑫ Merchants Hall

LEITH ST.

ST. JAMES' CENTRE

YORK PLACE

REGENT ROAD
CALTON RD.
WATERLOO PLACE

② ①

NORTH BRIDGE

N. ST.

③

S. ST.

ANDREW ST.

ST. ANDREW SQ.

ANDREW ST.

④

⑫

QUEEN ST.

THISTLE ST.

GEORGE ST.

ROSE ST.

HIGH ST.

MARKET ST.

⑪ E. PRINCES ST. GDNS.

⑨ ⑩

THE MOUND

⑤

FRED-ERICK ST.

CASTLE ST.

CHARLOTTE SQ.

PRINCES STREET

⑧ ST. GDNS.

W. PRINCES

THE CASTLE

⑥ ⑦

KING'S STABLES RD.

LOTHIAN ROAD

Route 6

PRINCES STREET

Princes Street is renowned far and wide, indeed to many, Princes Street *is* Edinburgh. Despite the fact that many people say, 'it is not what it used to be', Princes Street still retains many of the qualities which first made it an 'ornament to the kingdom'.

We begin our walk at the eastern entrance to the city and to Princes Street, in Waterloo Place in the shadow of the monuments on Calton Hill. Originally designed for access to a new jail across on Calton Hill, this development became part of a grandiose vision of the east end of the city. In the middle of Waterloo Place is Regent Bridge but it is only when you look down through the arches that you realise that you are actually on a bridge. This is because it is linked by pillars to the rest of the buildings to achieve a unified, but rather severely classical, facade.

Coming down to the traffic lights, on the left is the main Post Office. This was once the site of the old Theatre Royal, and the rapturous scenes which met the famous actress Mrs Sarah Siddons, on her visits and performances in Edinburgh. The building which you can see is in an Italianate style and was built in 1866 at a cost of £120,000. From here you can get a fine view across to Register House and appreciate its gracious symmetry, with its Corinthian pillars in the centre and corners topped by turrets and a cupola.

Designed by Robert Adam, the building was begun in 1774 as the first major construction in the New Town. Half-way through its construction, however, the building ran short of funds. It sat unroofed for 6 years, 'the most magnificent pigeon-house in Europe'. Luckily it was eventually finished by the architect Robert Reid and is now the public record office for Scotland containing, amongst other things, the Treaty of Union with England in 1707. The Register House was purpose-built with thick stone walls separating the rooms to prevent fire and heating to ward off damp. In front is a bronze statue of Wellington on his horse, appropriately pointing to Waterloo Place and the National Monument on Calton Hill, for both of these were dedicated to the dead of the Napoleonic wars of which Wellington was, of course, the famous victor. The statue was by Sir John Steele, hence the Edinburgh aphorism, 'The Iron Duke, in Bronze by Steele'.

Throughout the 19th century you would have looked across the road to see coaching offices and small hotels and pubs. Now instead, your view is dominated by the massive North British Railway Hotel opened in 1902 after the other buildings had been demolished. A massive building with 13 storeys and a clocktower of about 200 feet, its effect is heightened by the fact that beyond it Princes Street is free from buildings above street level. This feature was no accident but part of deliberate town planning and hard won. Princes Street was part of the original plan for the New Town and was designed as the south terrace, open-sided to the south. When one John Home started to build a workshop on the south side, there was an outcry which was only resolved when the House of Lords decided against Home and the south side was safe. As you walk along you should offer up a prayer to these vigilantes for it is the superb views to the south that really makes Princes Street unique and so beautiful.

As you walk down the right side you pass Woolworth's store on the site of the first house to be built in Princes Street by John Neale, a silk merchant, in 1769. For many years no rates were paid on this building, originally as an incentive to Neale to move to an area which was only just beginning to establish itself as a desirable place to live. Also on the site was No. 10 Princes Street, once the offices of Scott's publisher Archibald Constable, whose meteoric rise to fame and then disaster, brought Scott down with him.

Princes Street was originally to be called St Giles' Street, but when King George III heard of this he was horrified for St Giles' Street in London was a very undesirable locality. Consequently the street was named Prince's Street after the Prince Regent and eventually dropped the apostrophe to become Princes Street.

The buildings in Princes Street have also had a rather chequered history. Firstly, by the mid 19th century the houses had mainly been turned into shops and fine new shops were being built. Then in the 1960s most of these were demolished, prior to the enactment of an extraordinary scheme to create a parade of new shops linked by a walkway at the first floor. The plan was never put into practice but the damage was done. There are, however, a few of the old Edwardian and Victorian buildings left particularly at this end. Notice, for example, the Edwardian building housing the department store of R. W. Forsyth.

But the best known store in Princes Street is Jenners, a little further along. Built in 1895 by Sir William Hamilton Beattie, the building's exterior gets more and more wild and idiosyncratic as it reaches the top with a host of statues and carvings. Inside balustraded galleries run round the sides, very attractive to the eye but often confusing to the would-be shopper. The origins of this famous store are slightly less respectable than one might imagine. The story goes that in 1838, two young drapery assistants, Charles Kennington and Charles Jenner took the day off to go to the races at Musselburgh and were fired. A few weeks later they opened a new store, presumably on their winnings. It quickly grew into Scotland's biggest retail shop but in 1892 a fire destroyed the building. Three years later the present building was opened.

Across the road is the Scott Monument of which more later, but behind that you already have a fine view of the buildings of the Old Town along the ridge to the Castle.

Turn right at Hanover Street and walk past the Merchants' Hall, built in 1866 for the Company of Merchants. Notice the fine crest and the fanned design of the stone above the windows on the ground floor. Turn left down Rose Street. This was one of the intermediary streets of the New Town, designed for the tradesmen and servants who were to serve the richer folk in Princes Street and George Street on either side. Later it gained a reputation for the number of its pubs. Many of these have disappeared but you will find that by the time you have reached the next intersection with Frederick Street you will have already passed 4 pubs!

At the end of this part of Rose Street some of the old 18th century houses are still visible. Cross the road and continue along Rose Street which is now an attractive pedestrian precinct where new shop fronts succeed in harmonising with the original buildings. At the next crossroads you come to Castle Street where further up on the right No. 32 was the birthplace of Kenneth Grahame, author of *The Wind In The Willows* and the creator of the most famous toad in literature. You may wish to make a short detour to see this, otherwise turn left into Castle Street which, true to its name, provides an impressive sight of the Castle.

At the end turn right into Princes Street and at the junction with South Charlotte Street cross over to the other side of Princes Street and walk towards the church lying alongside the road. This is St John's Episcopalian Church which was built in 1817 by William Burn. It is distinguished by its 120 foot square tower and fine interior fan vaulting, in the style of St George's Chapel at Windsor. Buried in the churchyard are the portrait painter Sir Henry Raeburn, the novelist Catherine Sinclair and James Donaldson, the founder of the Donaldson Hospital for the deaf.

Walk back along Princes Street in the direction you came and go down the steps to the right of the church which lead to St Cuthbert's Church, parallel but behind St John's and standing on the site of the earliest church in the city built in the 8th century. The present church was erected in 1892 although its spire was part of an earlier 18th century church. In the churchyard are more famous graves, this time of the 'opium-eater' Thomas de Quincy and Alexander Napier of Merchiston, the inventor of Logarithms. At the south-west corner of the graveyard to the right is an old watchtower used in the early 19th century by bereaved relatives to guard their dead from the nefarious activities of grave-snatchers, of whom the most famous – or infamous – were Burke and Hare (see page 102).

Return to Princes Street, turn right and walk down the next but one flight of steps into West Princes Street Gardens.

As late as 1870, your entry to these gardens would have been barred by a forbidding notice:

Any person entering these gardens without a legal right will be prosecuted. No person permitted to lend a garden key.

for these were private and jealously guarded gardens. However, now as we walk, we have reason to thank the founders of these gardens. Before 1816, when the Princes Street Proprietors, i.e. all those with houses between Hope and Hanover Street, leased the land from the town, the area was, in the words of Lord Cockburn, 'a fetid and festering marsh, the receptacle for skinned horses, hanged dogs, frogs and worried cats'. This was the remains of the old Nor' Loch, formed in the 15th century to fortify the north side of the town.

The Proprietors spent £7,000 landscaping the gardens, providing paths and sheltered walks under the Castle, planting shrubs and flowers with the aim of providing a promenade where, 'genteel folk might walk at all times without risk of meeting improper persons'. In 1827, Sir Walter Scott was presented with a key to the Gardens and in his journal, he records how he used to walk from Castle Hill to the gardens, 'through a scene of grandeur and beauty perhaps unequalled whether the foreground or distant view is considered.'

Gradually the privilege of the gardens was encroached upon. By 1849, much to the horror of the Proprietors, the railway had been driven through the heart of the gardens, and bands were playing in the gardens. But 'lower orders' were still excluded, also nursemaids and children who disturbed the music, whilst sick people in wheelchairs had to show a medical certificate to prove that their disease was not contagious before they were let in. Finally, in 1876, the gardens were sold to the city and made open to all.

Walk towards the highly ornate fountain which was originally designed for the Paris Exhibition, and then given to Edinburgh in 1869 by a gunmaker, called Daniel Ross. Its many stages contain several depictions of womanhood and Dean Ramsay complained at the time that the statue at the top was immoral, but this complaint went unheeded!

Turn left and walk along the path parallel to Princes Street and you soon come to one of the many monuments in the gardens. This is a stone erected in 1978 by grateful Norwegians from the Second World War. Skirt round the rather ugly bandstand, built in 1935, and notice on the right the statue of a soldier gazing earnestly into the distance in front of a frieze of soldiers. This is named, 'The Call', and was put up by Americans of Scottish descent for Scottish soldiers who died in the First World War. As you walk back along the path parallel to the road, you pass another memorial, this time to the Royal Scots Greys, in the form of a soldier on horseback.

If the season is right (May to October), as you near the end of the gardens you will be able to enjoy the wonderful display of Edinburgh's Floral Clock. This is the oldest Floral Clock in the world; laid out in 1902 in the shape of a crown to mark King Edward VII's coronation, in 1904 it was converted into a clock but with only one hand. A year later, another hand and a cuckoo which makes an appearance every quarter of an hour was installed. Each year more than 20,000 plants are put in the zinc hands and surrounds to form a display which often takes a topical motif. For those who may be wondering where the clock's mechanics are, they are housed under the fine marble statue of Allan Ramsay, author of *The Gentle Shepherd*.

This statue by Steele, was originally intended to sit in front of Ramsay Lodge, the poet's curiously shaped house by the Castle, but the ground was not firm enough and so the statue was placed in its present site. Ramsay is shown in the business of composition with a book and pencil, and his robes of the day's fashion look, by our standards, more like night attire than day wear. Notice particularly his turban, looking for all the world like a silk nightcap. Behind Ramsay, towards the railway line, is the memorial to the Royal Scots put up in 1952, as a tribute to this Edinburgh based regiment. It is semi-circular in shape with blocks showing the changing dress and equipment of the regiment and its battle honours, whilst the bronze railing carries a quotation from the Declaration of Arbroath in 1320.

Leave the gardens and cross the Mound. Appropriately named, this road started life as a mound of earth and rubble, dumped from digging the foundations for the new houses in Princes Street. At one time, as many as 1,800 cartloads were being dumped here every day. Thus a shortcut was created between the Old and New Town which was nicknamed, 'Geordie Boyd's Mud Brig', after George Boyd, a Lawnmarket clothier, who was first to use it. Eventually a proper road was built at the request of the Lawnmarket traders but despite its undoubted usefulness, it did not meet with general approval. Walter Scott for instance, described the road as, 'that huge deformity which now extends its lumpish extent betwixt Bank Street and Hanover Street'.

In 1840, the Mound was changed from a straight road to a curved one to provide flat ground for the National Gallery of Scotland, designed by William Playfair in a classical style. Also by Playfair, but built much earlier, is the Royal Scottish Academy standing in front of the National Gallery. It was erected here in 1826 and then the exterior was elaborated and enriched by Playfair some 10 years later.

Walking round the side of the building, notice the sphinxes on the roof, while the front has a Doric portico and a huge statue of Queen Victoria.

Enter East Princes Street Gardens and to your left you can see two more statues. The first is of John Wilson, who, as 'Christopher North', played a vital part in the success of *Blackwoods Magazine*. This started life as a 'scandalous' magazine but it quickly achieved high literary renown. The second is of another literary figure, Adam Black, who founded the publishing company of A. & C. Black and was also Lord Provost of Edinburgh. But these statues pale into insignificance besides the most famous monument in Edinburgh, the Scott Monument, which has been likened to many things and perhaps most accurately, to a rocket awaiting blast off. It has been extravagantly praised and censured, finding disapproval, for example, with Dickens who thought it was a complete failure, 'resembling nothing so much as a gigantic Gothic church spire taken down and placed on the ground.'

The Monument was the work of George Meikle Kemp who was a self-taught architect but unfortunately, walking back one night to his home in Morningside, he fell into the Union Canal and died. The building was still in progress and his brother-in-law took over the construction. The statistics of the building are impressive: its foundations are based 52 feet below Princes Street on solid rock, it is about 200 feet high and has 287 steps, whilst all round the Monument in separate niches are 64 statuettes of characters from Scott's novels, such as Meg Merilees from *Guy Mannering*. Sitting under the spire is Scott himself, depicted by Sir John Steele at twice life size, writing, with his favourite dog Maida, at his side. The Monument took 6 years to build, between 1840–46 and cost £16,000. At one time funds were so low that special 'Waverley' Balls were held in London and Edinburgh to raise money.

For a small fee you can climb the Monument and it is well worth doing so, for the views are superb. But be warned, it is a steep and arduous climb and when you think you have reached the summit, at a small chapel-like enclosure, you have several more stages to go before you can say you have really reached the top. From all the vantage points the views are wonderful, with the Old Town to the south, the New Town to the north, and Calton Hill to the east, and beyond, the hills of Fife in one direction, the Pentland Hills in another.

Descend to the bottom and pass the last statue in the gardens which is of David Livingstone who started life in Lanarkshire and then went on to work as a missionary and explorer in Africa, the scene of his famous encounter with Stanley.

Waverley Bridge to the right leads to Waverley Station. The present building dates from 1897 but there were stations here as early as 1842 when the Edinburgh, Leith and Granton Railway opened their Canal Street Station slightly to the south of the present station; this was closed in the 1860s. In 1847 the North British Railway Company bought the Edinburgh–Glasgow Railway Company and in 1848 opened the General Station comprising the terminii of the Glasgow line and of their own Berwick route. The present station rejoices in a 13 acre glassroof which is designed to be below the level of Princes Street so safeguarding the views to the south.

Pass Waverley Steps, often a hazardous wind tunnel, and return to the North British Railway Hotel, the end of the walk.

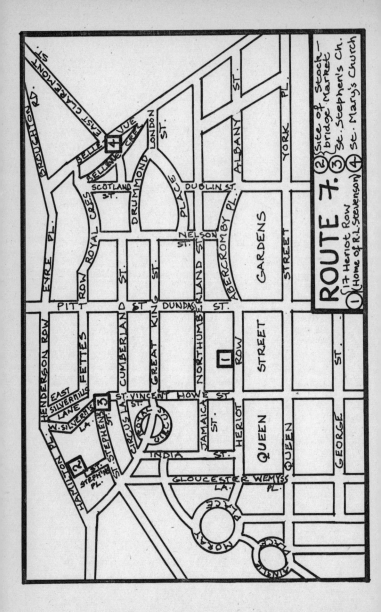

ROUTE 7.

① 17 Heriot Row (Home of R.L.Stevenson)
② Site of Stock-bridge Market
③ St. Stephen's Ch.
④ St. Mary's Church

Route 7

THE SECOND NEW TOWN

This walk explores more of the streets which were built as the trend to live in the fashionable New Town gathered momentum, or as Robert Louis Stevenson described it, the acceleration of 'the great exodus across the valley when the New Town began to spread abroad its draughty parallelograms, to rear its long frontage on the opposing hill'. As the author said, parallelograms were the chief feature of the New Town but because of its steep slopes the layout of the Second New Town was slightly less rigidly formal than in the First New Town, even if it was just as draughty!

Begin the walk in Heriot Row at the junction with Wemyss Place. This street, one of the first to be built in this area, was begun after about £3 million had already been spent on building the new Georgian town. The land belonged to the Trustees of Heriot Hospital, founded after the bequest of the rich jeweller and financier, 'Jinglin' Geordie' Heriot, after whom the street was thus indirectly named. Built between 1802 to 1808, the appearance of the street has since been altered with an extra floor having been added to many houses. But, enjoying views onto Queen Street Gardens, this is still one of the most attractive streets in the Second New Town.

As you walk along the street notice the way the houses are designed to look like one grand facade in a 'Palace-front' style of architecture. This was a new development first introduced by Robert Adam in Charlotte Square in the First New Town, and then widely adopted in the architecture of the Second New Town. The fine houses are punctuated at intervals with wrought iron lampstands which were usually erected after the houses had been built. There is also much solid gleaming brasswork to be seen, and should a door be open the view inside will, as likely as not, be of an interior as elegant and impressive as the exterior. Some of the houses are softened in appearance by creeper growing over the stone, this is an unusual sight in the New Town where greenery is mainly confined to formal gardens.

On the corner of India Street at No. 43, once lived William Playfair the architect who was responsible for many of the city's classical buildings. Cross Howe Street and look down the steep slope to St Stephen's Church. Continue along Heriot Row and stop at No. 17 and look at the plaque underneath the lampstand on the railings. On it are inscribed lines from Robert Louis Stevenson's poem, *The Lamplighter,* and it was here that the author and poet lived as a child. We are told how Stevenson, whose delicate health often left him an invalid, used to watch 'Leerie' the lamplighter from his bedroom as he came to light the lamps in the street. It is said that the young child gained inspiration for *Treasure Island* from the pond with an island in the middle, situated in the gardens opposite.

A little further along No. 13 was the first house to be built in the Second New Town. When the first inhabitants moved into the house they were considered to be 'out of the world' by the Queen Street residents who thought that civilisation stopped with their street which was the northern boundary of the First, and as far as they were concerned, the only New Town. In fact the building of Heriot Row at all was considered by many as mere reckless speculation.

No. 6 Heriot Row provided the home for another writer, Henry Mackenzie who was the author of a sentimental novel, *The Man of Feeling* which brought him much fame.

As you cross Dundas Street with its fine view to the Forth you might be tempted to agree with Robert Louis Stevenson who criticised the way the houses of the New Town were sited so that many of them 'face the wrong way, intent, like the Man with the Muck-Rake, on what is not worth observation', but then went on, 'perhaps it is all the more surprising to come suddenly on a corner and see . . . a mile or more of falling street, and beyond that . . . a blue arm of the sea and the hills upon the farther side'. Looking up to the south, notice the ingenious piece of town-planning where the spire of Tolbooth Church, on the line of Dundas Street, and the towers of New College look like one building.

We now come to Abercromby Place which is named after Sir Ralph Abercromby, victor of the Battle of the Pyramids. This was the first street to be built in the New Town in a curve and although it introduces a welcome variety in the layout of the streets, its shape was a matter of necessity rather than of design. A Queen Street proprietor refused to sell his land opposite and so the builders had to curve the street away from the intended line of the road. Lord Cockburn reported that the shape of the street was such a novelty that 'people used to go and stare at the curved street'.

Turn left into Nelson Street, another road with a naval flavour. Its tall tenements rather dwarf this small narrow street although there are some fine ironwork balconies, as for instance, those over the Nelson Hotel. Turn right into Northumberland Street, then pick up Nelson Street again to the left which takes you down to Drummond Place.

This was designed as the eastern end to the Second New Town just as St Andrew's Square closes the First New Town at the east. Its crescent shape is less formal than that of the square plan which it was originally designed to have. The architecture is in a 'Palace-front' style as before, and most of it was built from 1816 onwards, save for the eastern part which was built in 1806. Walk round in an anti-clockwise direction and look across to the gardens in the centre where up until 1845 you would have seen a grand house. This was Bellevue House built in the 18th century which eventually became the Excise Office. This house replaced a 16th century lodge which was lived in for many years by George Drummond who, as Lord Provost of Edinburgh, played a large part in the initial stages of creating a new Georgian town. The square was also named after him.

As you walk around notice the Ionic pilasters with the characteristic scrolls at the top, and the symmetrical design of the blocks of houses. Some of the houses such as those on the corner of Dundonald Street have been recently restored and look particularly attractive. Further along at No. 28 lived a gentleman called Charles Fitzpatrick Sharpe. A friend of Sir Walter Scott, he was famous for his witty gestures such as representing himself on a visiting card just by the musical notation for C Sharp, and also for the dandiness of his clothes. The famous novelist Sir Compton Mackenzie lived a little further along at No. 31.

Follow the square all the way round until you come to Great King Street. This was the main street in the Second New Town, and was named after George III, although the idea of putting a statue of the King at the west end of the street was never carried out. With its four identical blocks of houses this street clearly demonstrates the features of the 'Palace-front' design. As you walk along you can see that the centre and end houses are taller than those inbetween. These taller buildings were built as flats and together with the complete houses which made up the rest of the block provided a good variety of type and size of accommodation, although now, of course, most of the houses are subdivided as well.

Like the neighbouring streets, Great King Street has had its share of famous residents including J. M. Barrie, the creator of Peter Pan who lodged for a while at No. 3, the first entry or 'stair' on the left-hand side. A few doors down at No. 9, the 'opium-eater' De Quincy lived between 1830–34. Beyond Dundas Street and across the road at No. 60, lived a 19th century minister, the Reverend Edward Irving who was known for the length of his sermons and his Bible-readings, both of which must have tested the endurance of his congregation on occasions. No. 72 was the home of the painter Sir William Allan who apart from painting a portrait of Scott and his son, also painted scenes from exotic places such as Russia, Turkey and Eastern Europe. One of the last houses in the street, No. 84, was the home of Felix Yamewicz from 1823–1848. Despite being Polish by birth, this musician and composer was co-founder of the first Edinburgh Festival in 1815, as a precursor of the modern festival.

We now arrive at the gardens of the Royal Circus, one of the finest streets in the New Town. The two matching crescents are the more impressive for the fact that they were built in just over a year, between 1821–23. In fact Thomas Carlyle, who in 1821 had rooms in neighbouring Jamaica Street, was forced to move as the sound of the building was disturbing his studies. Turn left into South East Circus Place and bear round to the left of the crescent. Notice the fine ironwork balconies and finials at the top of the railings, although the facades of the houses are plainer here than before.

If you wish you can do a circular tour all the way round the Circus, otherwise, contenting yourself with a view of the other side through the gardens, join the axial road which runs through the development and turn left down North West Circus Place. This road leads down into Stockbridge but our walk forks to the right, by the sign of the pawnbrokers, into St Stephen Street. Originally called Brunswick Street and built between 1824–70, after a long period of neglect this street is beginning to see better times again, with a programme of work carried out by the Edinburgh New Town Conservation Committee.

A little way along the street turn left into St Stephen Place to see the last remnants of the old Stockbridge Market in the form of an arch proclaiming, 'Stockbridge Market, butcher, meat, fruits, fish, and poultry'. Opened in 1825, this was the first market in the New Town and it was the chief market area right up to the 20th century which saw the rival development of Broughton Market to the east. Returning to St Stephen Street notice the unusual feature of double-decked shops where steps lead up as well as down to shops.

At the end of the road you come to the most famous landmark of this part of town, St Stephen's Church, which is best seen if you walk up St Vincent Street a little way. Originally intended for a site in the Royal Circus, it was rumoured that the present position of the church was chosen by the city authorities who wanted to block the view of the Edinburgh Academy which was threatening to rival their new Royal High School on Calton Hill. Designed by William Playfair, the church is a curious looking building in the form of a diamond-like square. There are fine classical details on the facade and an impressive tower containing the clock which is reputed to have the longest pendulum in Europe, some say in the world. Notice the unusual device of placing the entrance in the gallery at the top of a long flight of steps. Observe also the way it sits astride a V-shape of roads, one of which, West

Silvermills Lane, is a reminder of the days when silver, brought from nearby Linlithgow, was milled here in the early 17th century.

Turn left into Cumberland Street, built in the 1830s, whose smaller-scale contrasts with the grand style of roads such as Great King Street. Turn left into Dundas Street and then first left into Fettes Row. This was designed to parallel Heriot Row as the outside terrace of the Second New Town, but it has suffered much more from the processes of decay and development than has its partner. The intended garden to the north on the right-hand side was never properly laid out and the ground was occupied instead by a tatty collection of small commercial premises. Gradually these are being replaced by higher quality modern buildings.

It is worth turning left and going right to the end of the row to see Nos. 23–24 which was the site of one of the first reconstruction works to be achieved through a New Town Conservation Committee grant. The houses have been completely refaced with new 'Classach' stone and now look delightful. A plaque in the wall records the visit of the Queen Mother in European Architectural Heritage Year, 1975.

Retrace your steps and cross over Dundas Street to the other part of Fettes Row. The houses on the right vary in quality, some have been cleaned up, for example No. 1, others are still rather shabby. Opposite are the offices of the Royal Bank whose new architecture clashes with that of the Georgian houses.

Fettes Row takes you into the Royal Crescent where the style of architecture changes with the introduction of heavy Doric porches. The effect is less pleasing than in the Royal Circus, particularly as the fine balconies tend to look rather lost between the giant pillars. Like Fettes Row, Royal Crescent suffers from the messy development of the north side in place of the garden which never materialised. On the south side the houses have rather a neglected appearance but reconstruction work is presently going on in some houses so this situation may improve.

At the end of the crescent look back to a fine view of St Stephen's Church. Turn right into Cornwallis Place and right again into Bellevue Crescent. This elegant crescent is virtually symmetrical despite the north and south sides either side of the church being built at different times and by different architects. The first section, the northern one, was built by Thomas Bonnar in 1819–32, the second by David Cousin in 1882, although modelled on the lines of the original design. Notice the giant Ionic pilasters on the facade of the houses and then step back to fully admire the focal point of the crescent which is St Mary's Church, built in 1824. Notice its huge Corinthian pillars forming a grand portico and the very attractive tiered steeple with its pointed dome.

Continue round the crescent and turn right into Mansfield Place which was built by Thomas Bonnar in 1820. Turn right into London Street, a toned down, but nonetheless elegant, version of Great King Street. Notice the delicate iron balconies on the right and return to Drummond Place, the end of the walk.

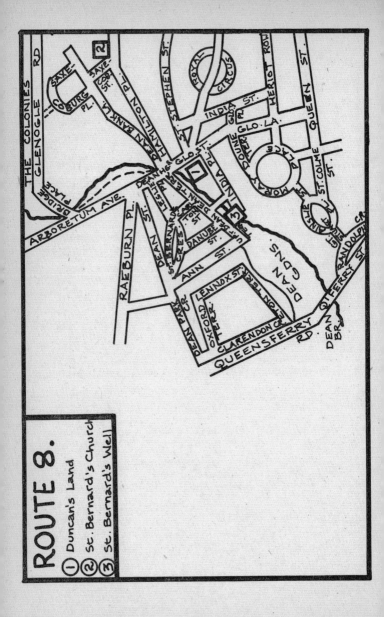

ROUTE 8.

① Duncan's Land
② St. Bernard's Church
③ St. Bernard's Well

THE COLONIES
GLENOGLE RD
COLOGNE PLACE
SAXE COBURG PL.
SAXE COBURG ST.
HAMILTON PL.
DEAN BANK LA.
No.2
ST. STEPHEN ST.
ROYAL CIRCUS
INDIA ST.
GLO. PR. ST.
GLO. LA.
HERIOT ROW
GLENFINLAS ST.
QUEEN ST.
DOUNE TER.
MORAY PL.
ST. COLME ST.
ALBYN PL.

BRIDGE PLACE
ARBORETUM AVE.
RAEBURN PL.
DEAN ST.
GLO. ST.
ST. BERNARD'S CRES.
CARLTON ST.
DEAN TER.
DANUBE ST.
DEAN PK. ST.
INDIA PL.
No.1
No.3
ANN ST.
LENNOX ST.
LEON TERR.
DEAN GDNS
GLENFINLAS ST.
AINSLIE PL.
RANDOLPH CR.

DEAN PARK CR.
OXFORD TERR.
CLARENDON CR.
QUEENSFERRY RD
QTFERRY ST.
DEAN BR.

78

Route 8

THE MORAY ESTATES
AND STOCKBRIDGE

This walk takes you through one of the most delightful parts of the New Town where grand crescents sit side by side with rural, almost wild, scenery.

Beginning at the top of Queensferry Street, turn right into Randolph Crescent just as the road slopes down towards Dean Bridge. You have now entered what was once the suburban estate of the Earl of Moray but which became the grandest private housing development in the New Town. From the outset it was intended as an exclusive estate and, still predominantly residential, it remains one of the city's most prestigious areas.

When the Earl of Moray decided to sell rights to build on his land in 1822, he laid down rigid standards of design which only a rich man could fulfill. The entire estate was to conform to a design by the architect James Gillespie Graham. This was true not only of the main buildings, 5 guineas being required before the new proprietor could get a copy of these plans, but also of the stables, pavements, sewers, and even the railings. Thus, the architecture and ironwork of Randolph Crescent sets the tone for the succeeding streets.

Walk round the crescent to the right and turn right into Great Stuart Street which links the developments of the Moray Estate. Like the other streets its name is connected with the Earl of Moray: Stuart was his family name while Randolph as in Randolph Crescent was his Christian name. Ainslie Place which we now enter was named after the family into which the Earl married. In this street we can see Gillespie

Graham's plan working itself out as it makes use of the awkward shapes and terrain of this part of the city. The architecture is the same as in Randolph Crescent, being in a 'Palace-front' style with groups of houses making up a unit which is designed to look like one grand house. The only difference is that here the facade of the houses has to bend more round the gracious lines of the street.

Walk round on the left, looking across the road to see the houses between the trees in the middle. The other side is almost identical except that it is divided up by a street. As you walk around notice the fine iron work, particularly the details of the railings, many as they were originally designed with wreath designs between the rails. Outside many houses there are also old wrought iron lampstands sitting astride the railings. Turn left to pick up St Stuart Street again which takes you into the climax of the development.

Moray Place is actually 12 sided and the grandiose facade is made to bend round curves and rise up and down according to the lie of the land. The result may be a little curious but it is undoubtedly impressive. Walk round the square to the left and notice the style of architecture with a Tuscan portico of eight pillars at the centre of each block of houses. Nearly all the houses are now broken up into flats or houses but their facades remain as grand as ever. Some have fine fanlights divided up by astragals (bars) which lend small touches of elegance and individuality to the buildings.

Take the first left fork into Doune Terrace. This is a very handsome road with houses on one side allowing fine views to the left. In the New Town it is an unusual sight to see houses turned towards the scenery for usually, as in Moray Place, they face away from it. From the bottom you can look across to Lord Moray's pleasure gardens at the back of Moray Place, which give the fortunate residents access to beautiful gardens and a cliffside walk. At No. 1, the last house before Doune Terrace turns into Gloucester Place, lived Robert Chambers of dictionary and publishing fame.

Turn left and walk down the steep Gloucester Street into Stockbridge. This road used to be called Church Street as it was the route taken by the inhabitants of Stockbridge, for a long time a distinct village, on their way to St Cuthbert's Church at the West End of Princes Street. On the right-hand side of the road on the corner of India Place, is Duncan's Land, an attractive stone house completely different from the grand architecture of Moray Place. This house, the birthplace of the painter David Roberts, was built of stone taken from a house demolished in the Lawnmarket when Bank Street was created. As an indication of how rural this area once was, Duncan's Land was built for Henry Duncan in 1746 as his country house.

Turn right into Hamilton Place. The atmosphere is again entirely different with mainly Victorian buildings such as the Library and Salvation Army Hall and the fine school. Turn left into Saxe-Coburg Street and walk past St Bernard's Church which was built in 1823 by James Milne and enter Saxe-Coburg Place where on the corner on the right was once a china factory. As proof of this, a teapot and 2 cups and saucers made at the factory can be seen in the Royal Scottish Museum in Chambers Street.

Like St Bernard's Church the U-shaped Saxe-Coburg Place was built in the 1820s but it was never completed, and if you walk round you will notice that the northern end is a little spoilt by Glenogle Baths, jutting up from the road below.

Just past the baths turn left down a winding path which brings you out at the Colonies. These are sets of

19th century terraces containing artisan housing. Turn left and bear round into Bridge Place and cross the bridge. Take the steps to the left of the bridge which are clearly marked as the Water of Leith Walkway. Walk down the path which although urban rather than rural in flavour provides a welcome break from the busy roads. The path ends just short of another bridge, Stockbridge. Climb the steps to the road again.

Although this bridge is named, 'Stockbridge', it was an earlier wooden bridge which gave the village its name, since 'stock' means wood. The river flowing underneath provided the focus for a host of small industries such as mills, tanneries and the china factory mentioned above. In 1785 a wider stone bridge was needed for easier access, although even the one which was built then, was too narrow and rose in the middle and later had to be widened and levelled.

From here you can look across to the right to the building which once served as Stockbridge's church. The church was composed of stones taken from the old Free Church of St George's in Lothian Road, demolished in the 1860s when Princes Street Station, now closed, was built. Now in its turn the church has changed its use and in 1981 was being converted into homes for the elderly. However, its distinctive tower which was built from spare stones from the Lothian Road church when the Stockbridge church was erected, is being retained.

From the bridge cross the street into Dean Terrace. This was one of the streets started in 1817 when the painter Henry Raeburn decided to lease his lands which were greatly increased after his marriage to Ann, widow of Count Leslie and owner of old Deanhaugh House. It was intended to build Nos. 10–15 as a mirror image of Nos. 1–6 with a higher central block. But development proceeded very slowly, grand ideas of design had to be abandoned, and gaps were left between Nos. 6–11 until 1879, when they were filled in after the re-development of the estate of old Deanhaugh House. But whatever its original aspirations this is one of the most attractive streets in the New Town with fine views over to the pleasure gardens of Moray Place and an enviable river-side position.

Turn first right into Carlton Street. This was once the site of St Bernard's House, home of an 18th century lawyer or Writer to the Signet, Mr Walter Ross. By all accounts he developed a very effective way of keeping out unwanted intruders. Having set man-traps to no avail, Ross got hold of a leg from the Royal Infirmary, dressed it up in a stocking and shoe and sent it through the city by the town crier who showed it to the public, proclaiming that it had been found in Mr Ross's grounds who now wanted to return the leg to its rightful owner. From then on Ross was left in peace!

Carlton Street is now an elegant road with long balconies curving gracefully round to take you into St Bernard's Crescent. This grand street must once have looked very incongruous for, when it was originally built in 1824, it was set in open country. Now of course, all the surrounding lands are built up but the crescent retains an open air.

Cross Leslie Place, named after Count Leslie, the one-time owner of Deanhaugh House which used to stand here and walk round the Crescent in an anti-clockwise direction. Notice the way the smaller pillars on Nos. 3–17 grow up to become giant Doric ones at No. 17. The following houses are the centrepiece of the development and the pillars are so large they almost dwarf the front doors. At No. 29 once lived Leith Richie, writer and editor of the *Edinburgh Journal,* and also a companion to the artist Turner, on his travels throughout Europe. After No. 35, the style changes with Victorian houses and new houses on the corner. Cross the road and, noticing the way in which the pattern of houses repeats itself just beyond Danube Street, turn right down this road. Parallel, and similar in design to Carlton Street, this road takes you back to the river and Dean Terrace which now becomes Upper Dean Terrace.

This part of Dean Terrace was once called Mineral Street and if you look across the river, just before the road ends, you will see why. Through the trees you can see a statue nestling under a classical dome. This is St Bernard's Well, very popular at the end of the 18th century for the professed health-giving powers of its mineral waters. The well was designed by Alexander Nasmyth in 1789 while the figure of Hygeia, Goddess of Health, was added later in 1888. To see the well more closely take the walk through the Dean Village, (page 121).

St Bernard's Well and Dean Gardens by the river were specifically designed to create a rural setting in town, and the result is one of the most beautiful parts of Edinburgh. But leaving the river behind turn right into Ann Street. Like the other roads this street was once part of Henry Raeburn's estate and was probably named after his wife, Ann Leslie. This was only fair since much of Raeburn's estate came to him through his marriage to Ann, a wealthy widow and some years his senior.

This is an enchanting street softened by the plentiful front gardens and foliage, and varying lines of architecture undulating now towards, now away from the line of the street. It is thought to have been largely designed by Raeburn himself and reflects his concern for creating a countryside effect in the city. As one commentator said, it begins like a village street which develops into a 'Greek Temple in a cottage garden'.

As you walk along you can see what this writer meant with neat small houses gradually giving way to a grand centrepiece of classical proportions. The houses bend round to meet Dean Park Crescent into which we should now turn left.

This pleasant road of bow windows and slate roofed houses has no houses on the left bank which rises steeply. At the end of the road you can either turn left into the elegant Clarendon Crescent or double back on yourself into Oxford Terrace. It is well worth doing the latter for you soon have a lovely view over the beautiful gardens around the Water of Leith. Follow the road round through Lennox Street and into Eton Terrace, which takes you back onto Queensferry Street, at the junction with Clarendon Crescent.

Turn left and walk over the Dean Bridge designed by Thomas Telford in 1832, towering 106 feet high over the water. Surprisingly, this superb bridge was built, not to carry the road northwards which is now its main function, but to provide access to the houses and streets across the river. These roads, such as Eton and Oxford Terrace, were eventually built on the land of Lord Provost Learmouth who paid most of the cost of the bridge.

Standing on the bridge you have a marvellous view to the left of the gardens tumbling down to the river, while to the right you look down to the Dean Village. Despite the splendour of the spot this used to be a favourite place for suicides. Such was the concern about this problem that in 1888, it was decided to raise the height of the parapet and put spikes on the top to make jumping more difficult.

Continue on up Queensferry Street which takes you past the entrance to Randolph Crescent and eventually back to the West End.

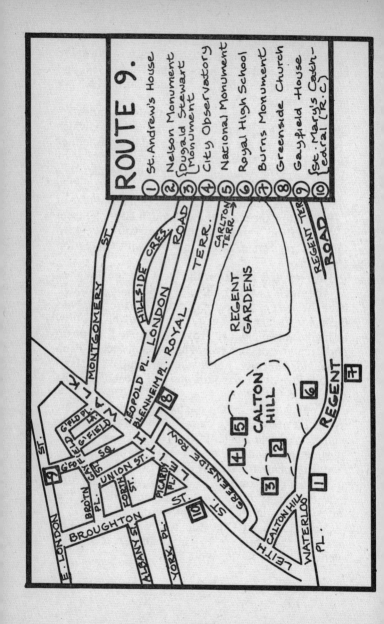

ROUTE 9.

① St. Andrew's House
② Nelson Monument
③ Dugald Stewart Monument
④ City Observatory
⑤ National Monument
⑥ Royal High School
⑦ Burns Monument
⑧ Greenside Church
⑨ Gayfield House
⑩ St. Mary's Cath- edral (R.C.)

REGENT GARDENS

CALTON HILL

MONTGOMERY ST.
HILLSIDE CRES.
LONDON ROAD
LEOPOLD PL.
BLENHEIM PL.
ROYAL TERR.
CARLTON TERR.
REGENT TERR.
REGENT ROAD
REGENT

GAYFIELD SQ.
GEO. GAYFIELD PL.
GAYFIELD ST.
BROTN PL.
UNION ST.
FORTH ST.
PICARDY PL.
GREENSIDE ROW
LEITH ST.
WATERLOO PL.
CALTON HILL
YORK PL.
ALBANY ST.
BROUGHTON ST.
E. LONDON ST.

86

Route 9

CALTON HILL

In the 19th century it became fashionable to think of Edinburgh as a modern Athens and in this walk we shall see how this came about, and witness its results.

Begin at the bottom of Calton Hill, a steep slope winding up from Leith Walk opposite the St James Hotel. This was once the only access to the hill above from which it takes its name. As you climb you have a fine view over to the docks and smoking chimneys of the port of Leith. On the left No. 14, under construction in 1981, is on the site of the home in later life of Burn's 'Clarinda', Mrs Agnes McLehose. At the top of the hill on the left is Rock House, once the home of David Octavius Hill, famous artist and photographer. After the small-scale domestic buildings of Calton Hill we are now confronted with grand, solemn architecture to the left and right.

To the right are the austere classical facades of Waterloo Place and Regent Bridge, built in 1815–16 to provide access to the new jail, which once stood on the site opposite you. The massive building which now stands there, St Andrew's House was built in 1939 by T. S. Tait a year after the jail was demolished. Now inhabited by a much more respectable class of people, this building was originally intended to house most of the Scottish Office including the office of the Secretary of State for Scotland. This particular office, however, has forsaken this grand site and now occupies new St Andrew's House in the St James Centre below.

Cross the road to have a closer look and notice its geometrical, almost Egyptian design. Above the entrance are statues of five Scottish saints and a carving of the Royal Coat of Arms, while paired unicorns are to be seen over the bottom windows to the right and left of the central block. Go to the right where you can see a turreted building, resembling a toy fortress, which was the governor's house from the days of the Calton jail.

Opposite the sight of the curious buildings on the hill may by now be whetting your appetite to climb up and see them more closely, so cross back over the road. For those who wish there is a gentler path up further along the road, but otherwise take the steps leading up the hill to the left, just opposite St Andrew's House. But before you start to climb note the medallions in the rock, commemorating three famous Scottish singers, Templeton, Wilson and Kennedy.

Fork right up the second flight of steps and you soon come to the top where a marvellous array of buildings dotted on the summit meet the eye. The best view of these buildings and the finest view of Edinburgh is to be had from the Nelson Monument, the first building you come to on the right. This curious building with its pentagonal base and battlemented tower, like an extended telescope, is Edinburgh's homage to the victor of the Battle of Trafalgar in 1805.

Look up to the flagstaff where every year on 21st October, the anniversary of Trafalgar, naval flags fly Nelson's famous message: 'England expects that every man will do his duty'. The flagstaff was once used to mark the arrival of the London steamer at Leith, and when Queen Victoria came to visit the city in 1842, this flag was supposed to advise the authorities of the Royal arrival. But a flag could not be found in time and the Queen was in the city before the waiting reception party, now very red-faced, knew she had even arrived! At the top of the tower is a small ball which drops in time with the one o'clock gun at the Castle. This was originally intended as a time-check for the sailors in Leith.

For a small fee you can climb to the top of the tower, providing you are fit for it is an arduous climb, but the view is superb. As Robert Louis Stevenson remarked, 'of all places for a view, this Calton Hill is perhaps the best, since you can see the Castle which you lose from the Castle and Arthur's Seat which you cannot see from Arthur's Seat'. You do indeed have a panoramic view over the whole of Edinburgh, New and Old towns, over to Leith and across to the hills of Fife, whilst to the east the Lothian coast stretches round to Gullane Point. This vantage point also gives an excellent view over the Calton Hill monuments which we will examine more closely after our descent.

At the base of the tower turn left towards the canon whose inscription indicates its chequered history. Originally owned by the Spanish administering Portugal, it was captured by the Burmese in their conquest of Arakan in 1784. The British later captured it and presented the canon to Edinburgh for their International Exhibition in 1886. It now points to the Castle but the story goes that it used to point to Princes Street further to the right. One night it was mysteriously moved and since a group of officials could not shift it the canon stayed where it was.

Walk over to the small domed temple on the left, which is a monument dedicated to Dugald Stewart, Professor of Moral Philosophy at Edinburgh University. A classical structure, it is based on the monument to Lysicrates on the Acropolis in Athens.

Go round the monument and walk over to the curious gothic building to the right. This, the oldest building on the hill, was erected in 1792 as an observatory. But there were insufficient funds for equipment and it was never used as such, soon being replaced by the large City Observatory to the right. Best seen from above, this is another classical building containing a central green dome surrounded by four porticoes. This was built by William Playfair in 1818 and served as the Royal Observatory from 1822 to 1897. To the right of the wall notice Playfair's monument to his uncle, the mathematician Professor John Playfair, another Greek building in the form of a temple.

By now it is becoming hard to escape the strong Greek influence in the architecture on Calton Hill, and this influence is most strongly expressed in the collection of columns to the right of the Observatory, the National Monument. By the 19th century, Edinburgh with a similar geographical position to Athens, in relation to the hills and sea, and enjoying a cultural revival was beginning to see itself as the 'Athens of the North'. Therefore when it was decided to build a national memorial to the dead of the Napoleonic wars a model of the Athenian Parthenon was chosen.

The foundation stone was laid in 1822 but funds were a great problem, work progressed very slowly and by 1830 only 12 columns had been erected. The money finally ran out and work was abandoned. Its unfinished form has led it to be nicknamed 'Edinburgh's Disgrace' and there have been numerous schemes to finish it, including creating a monument to Robert Burns, to Queen Victoria or turning it into a National Gallery. But nothing ever happened and it is hard to imagine Edinburgh's skyline without its distinctive silhouette looking more like the real Parthenon than it would do if it were ever completed.

Come away from the Monument and follow the road beyond the Monument which bends round to the right. On your left are the Regent Gardens, designed by Joseph Paxton, architect of the Crystal Palace, which lie inbetween the terraces we are now going to visit. The road leads down towards Regent Road again.

Dominating the road on the left is a massive, classically styled building, built in 1825–1829 to house the Royal High School. Designed by Thomas Hamilton with Greek Doric Pillars it looks more like a temple than a school. In 1979 the building was restored and converted to house the Scottish Assembly but as the Assembly did not then materialise it has been turned into law courts.

Also designed by Hamilton is the building across the road, the Burns Monument, also in Greek style. The surrounding pillars are decorated with lyres and lions' heads but the statue of Burns has been removed and now stands in the entrance hall of the Scottish National Portrait Gallery.

Taking the road to the left, Regent Terrace, we enter the complex of terraces, all by Playfair, but influenced by the ideas of Stark and his stress on the importance of adapting the buildings to the site. The resulting terraces, with their fine iron balconies and lampstands, graciously bend and cling to the contours on one side and have fine views to the open right side.

No. 3 is now the American Consulate whilst No. 10 once housed a number of distinguished men including Milton's biographer, David Mason, who was often visited by Dickens and Thackeray, and Alexander Bruce the founder of the Royal Geographical Society whose inaugural speech was delivered by the explorer, David Livingstone. No. 25 was the home of Alan Stevenson, uncle of Robert Louis Stevenson and the builder of the Skerryvore Lighthouse.

The curve in the line of the houses and the change to individual rounded balconies denotes Calton Terrace where you can catch glimpses of the sea between the trees. With Royal Terrace the style changes again with arched windows and colonnaded houses, Ionic to the sides with a Corinthian block in the middle. This north-facing terrace is the longest continuous block in the city. The east end of the city never became as fashionable as the west end but because of its view over Leith, this road was populated for a time by rich merchants who liked to be able to watch their ships coming into the harbour.

Royal Terrace takes you down to Greenside Parish Church on the left. Built by Gillespie Graham in 1838 in a mixture of classical and gothic styles, this church has close connections with the Stevenson family. The author Robert Louis Stevenson often worshipped here, describing the church in *Random Memories*, while a plaque commemorates his father and two brothers who gave land for a chapel.

This area of Greenside (looking down to the left) has a memorable history: from the 15th century onwards it was used as a tournament ground and it is rumoured that this was where Mary, Queen of Scots, first met her third husband, Bothwell, in 1554. In 1520 a Carmelite monastery was established which later became a leper hospital governed by strict rules. For example, if a leper opened the gate between sunrise and sunset he would be executed, such was the public fear of contamination. The road descends steeply to Blenheim Place, designed as one of the grand entrances to the Calton Estate.

From here you can walk back up Leith Walk but if you wish to continue further there are several interesting houses in the development across Leith Walk. Cross London Road into Elm Row noting the same colonnaded cornerpiece as in Blenheim Place. Cross Leith Walk and turn left into Gayfield Square.

Built at the turn of the 19th century, the effect of this square is rather ruined by the modern police station on the left. Walk down the right side noticing the way the plain architecture is ornamented only by the occasional wrought iron balcony. Turn right into Gayfield Square and at the end of the Street, standing out from its modern surroundings, is the superb Gayfield House. A lovely stone house with Dutch gables, it is surprising to realise that this was built as a country house in 1763–65 for its setting is now truly urban.

Retrace your steps back to Gayfield Square and turn right, and then right again, into Broughton Place. Look up to the left at the sign of the public bath house with a tall chimney behind it and notice also the fine Victorian church hall on the corner. On the right of Broughton Place is Broughton Place Church, a classical building with Doric columns set slightly off square from the road, and built in 1820–21 by the designer of Waterloo Place, Archibald Elliot. This row is built in the 'Palace-front' style common in much of the New Town, with the houses making up one unit dominated by a centrepiece taller than the rest.

The junction with Broughton Street is marked by curious turrets on three corners. Turn left and walk up the street. Just beyond Albany Street on the right-hand side of the road is an elegant chapel which is now in secular use. Notice the domestic style of its facade where the windows are in line with those in the surrounding houses. Broughton Street brings you out to Picardy Place which was once the site of a colony of French weavers. It was also the birthplace in 1859 of Sir Arthur Conan Doyle, the creator of the famous detective, Sherlock Holmes.

From here you can walk up Leith Street to the town centre noticing the Roman Catholic Cathedral on your right. First built in 1813 by James Graham, it has been much altered since and its exterior now looks quite modern.

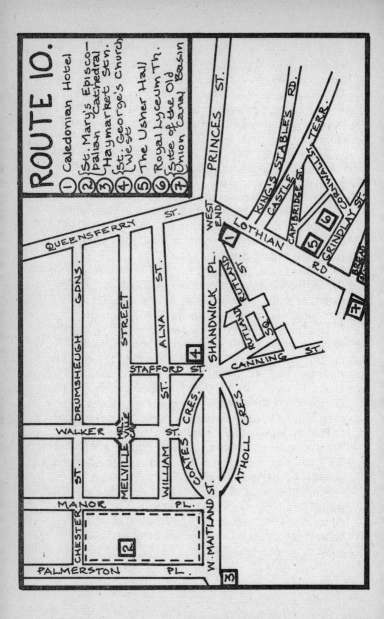

ROUTE 10.

① Caledonian Hotel
② { St. Mary's Episco-
     palian Cathedral
③ { Haymarket Scn.
④ { St. George's Church
     West
⑤ The Usher Hall
⑥ Royal Lyceum Th.
⑦ { Site of the Old
     Union Canal Basin

PRINCES ST.

WEST END

QUEENSFERRY   ST.

LOTHIAN

KING'S STABLES RD.

CASTLE ST.

CAMBRIDGE ST.

CORNWALL ST. TERR.

RD.

BREAD

⑥

⑤

⑦

①

DRUMSHEUGH GDNS.

STREET

ALVA   ST.

SHANDWICK PL.

RUTLAND ST.

RUTLAND SQ.

RUTLAND ST.

CANNING   ST.

STAFFORD ST.

④

WALKER   ST.

MELVILLE   ST.

WILLIAM   ST.

ST.

COATES CRES.

ATHOLL CRES.

MANOR   PL.

CHESTER   ST.

②

W. MAITLAND ST.

PALMERSTON   PL.

③

94

Route 10

THE WESTERN NEW TOWN

The western extension of the New Town is one of the most unsung parts of this development. Although this may be due to its proximity to the noisy West End, this neglect is unfair for it contains some very fine streets and the city's largest church, St Mary's Cathedral.

Start your walk at the bottom of Lothian Road, at the corner of the Caledonian Hotel which was opened in 1903, in conjunction with the new Princes Street Station, opened in 1894. The rather grimy exterior of the hotel contrasts with its plush interior. Turn left along the front of the hotel into Rutland Street. To the side of the hotel was the old entrance to the station, now demolished. Continue on the street which takes you into Rutland Square. This was planned by Archibald Elliot in 1819 but when building began in 1830, different plans were used by John Tait for the future Lord Provost Learmouth.

The exteriors of the houses have been blackened by soot from the old railway although some buildings have been cleaned up. Notice the Corinthian pillars on the houses as you enter the square and Ionic porches on the rest of the buildings. Walk clockwise around the square passing the offices of the intriguingly named, 'Royal Society for the Relief of Indigent Gentlewomen of Scotland,' a society redolent of earlier, more genteel, days, until you come to the grandest house in the square which is now the H.Q. of the R.A.C.

Follow this side of the road round into Canning Street which soon brings you out into the wide and spacious Shandwick Place, a few yards from the West

End. As late as 1800 the western limit of Princes Street formed the boundary of the built up city. Beyond this, where you are now standing, was the settlement of Kirkbraehead which stood at the top of two steep roads leading from Dean Village and Stockbridge, which the villagers had to climb to attend services at St Cuthbert's at the West End. The final destination of this route, at the church, explains the name of the village. But its days were numbered and at the beginning of the 19th century it was decided to build Shandwick Place in its stead.

This decision was part of the desire to build an imposing entrance to the west end of the city. Most of the development for this plan took place to the south of Shandwick Place and was based around the estate of the Walker family. Seeing that the trend in the New Town was to move westwards Sir Patrick Walker feued or leased his lands for development at the beginning of the 19th century. The overall plan was drawn up by Gillespie Graham but it seems that the Walker family miscalculated the trend in house fashion and the grand design, stretching all the way to the river to the north, developed very slowly. However, other landowners began to take up the idea and by 1815 streets were beginning to appear. One of these, Stafford Street, can by reached by crossing Shandwick Place and carrying straight on.

Stafford Street was built between 1819–25 to the plans or elevations of Robert Brown. Apart from the church on the right-hand side, this street contains small-scale housing. Unfortunately, shops built out from the line of the houses tend to spoil the harmony of the street.

Turn right into Alva Street, designed by Gillespie Graham, which is grander and less altered than Stafford Street. Notice the attractive semi-circular balconies which are the same as those in the development around Moray Place to the North. This is hardly surprising for the architect was the same in both cases. Turn left into Queensferry Street and first left into Melville Street.

This long, spacious street was the heart of Gillespie Graham's design and has since been given more authority by St Mary's Cathedral at the end, whose spires provide a fine vista down the street. Melville Street was designed by Robert Brown who also planned Stafford Street, and was mainly built between 1825–6. The majority of the houses have identical simple facades with slightly geometrical balconies, jutting out in the middle. A touch of distinction is added by the arched wrought iron lamp holders over many doors.

At No. 12 on the right, lived Mrs Henry Siddons, the daughter-in-law of the celebrated actress, Mrs Sarah Siddons. Her husband, Henry, helped by Scott's influence, secured a patent to stage performances at the Theatre Royal, where the main Post Office now stands in Waterloo Place. His wife was no mean actress, according to Scott, she performed her parts 'with much truth, feeling and tenderness'.

The grandest house in the street, No. 25, stands opposite Stafford Street and was the town house of the Walker family, the owners of the estate. Taller than its neighbours, its first and second floors are linked by Ionic columns while the ground floor has arched windows. After this house the buildings revert to their simpler style of architecture.

Slightly further along on the right, at No. 29, is the former home of Rev. Andrew Thomson, in his own time, the most popular preacher in Edinburgh, to such an extent he persuaded the fashionable residents of the New Town to start going to church again. Lockhart, Scott's biographer, was assured that 'church going was a thing completely out of fashion among the fine folks of the New Town till this man was removed from a church he formerly held in the Old Town, and established under the splendid dome of St George's'.

Melville Crescent forms a fitting break before the climax of the road at St Mary's Cathedral. The Crescent which was added later than the rest of the street, in 1855–56, is not really a crescent at all. In fact it is an octagonal form and as such is unique in Scotland. Notice the slightly more ornate form of design with lintels over the windows and colonnaded facades on some of the houses.

The statue in the centre is of Robert, Second Viscount Melville, after whom Melville Sound was named, in recognition of the Viscount's interest in Arctic exploration.

Walk up the street until you are in the shadow of St Mary's Episcopalian Cathedral. Note the gothic style of its architecture which is in complete contrast with the simple classical lines of Melville Street. Somehow this does not seem to matter: the Cathedral appears to enhance rather than spoil the appearance of the street. From here you can get a good view of the central tower of the Cathedral and can appreciate the finely balanced construction of the building, which supports and yet is not squashed by the enormous tower, which with its spire weighs 5,000 tons.

To get to the main entrance turn left into Manor Place, cross the road and walk down the path to the left of the Cathedral. At the end of the path turn right into Palmerston Place, walk past the Cathedral and cut up through the car park to look at Easter Coates House next door. This house was built in 1615 as the country home of Sir John Byers of Coates, and it is greatly to the credit of Gilbert Scott, the architect of the Cathedral, that he suggested it be allowed to stay and not be demolished as had been proposed. It is a very fine house with projections out to the sides. In the front of the building are two inscribed stones which, together with the unusual window with a double casement, were taken from the French Ambassador's Chapel, when it was demolished to make way for the building of George IV Bridge at the beginning of the 19th century.

Go back to the road and cross Palmerston Place to the traffic island opposite the Cathedral. From this vantage point you can appreciate its facade and can see that the Cathedral answered the demands that it should be 'in a handsome and substantial style of architecture'. This was stipulated by Barbara and Mary Walker, sisters of Sir Patrick Walker who was responsible for Melville Street and other surrounding streets. The two sisters were most concerned that there should be a fitting church for the Episcopalians who had been sorely neglected since the Glorious Revolution of 1688 had swept in Presbyterianism and put the old denomination, with its bishops, under severe pressure. By 1870 when the eldest sister, Mary, died, sufficient funds were available to fulfil their dreams. Sir Gilbert Scott, grandfather of the architect of Liverpool Cathedral, won a competition for the design. The foundation stone was laid on 21st May, 1874, and the Cathedral was finally consecrated on 29th October, 1879.

With its gothic magnificence it is not always easy to see the basis of the Cathedral's design which was in a cruciform plan with a central tower and spire. The two twin towers, slightly smaller than the central one, were built later, during the first World War and were named after Barbara and Mary, the Cathedral's benefactresses. Cross the road to see some of the Cathedral's fine detail, noticing the ornate doorway with its intricate ironwork and the multi-layered arch. Under this is a figure of Christ with the Key of

Heaven and a lamb, which alone took three months to complete.

The interior, as one might imagine from the style of the building, is lofty and spacious which is how Scott wanted it. The erection of this Cathedral, the first in Scotland after the Reformation, was a significant event and the architect wanted the grandeur of his design to reflect this. Even now it is the second largest church, after St Mungo's in Glasgow, in Scotland.

With your back to the Cathedral turn right down Palmerston Place which takes you past the curious looking Church of Scotland, built in 1862. Notice its arcaded front and twin towers, very different from the normal forms of ecclesiastical architecture. You soon come out into West Maitland Street and if you look to your right you can see Haymarket Station. Built in 1842, this was the original terminus of the Edinburgh and Glasgow Railway, until the railway line was extended through Princes Street to Waverley Station in 1846. This station building has been the oldest working one in Britain but in 1981 is threatened with demolition.

Turn left and enter Coates Crescent, one of the two crescents which give Shandwick Place an air of elegance at this point. Across the road, the houses of Atholl Crescent have Ionic columns on their facades. The style is simpler in Coates Crescent although each unit of houses has a grander block in the middle. The statue in the gardens opposite Walker Street is of Gladstone and is ornamented by smaller figures depicting such attributes as eloquence and vitality.

At the end Coates Crescent takes us back onto Shandwick Place. This is named after Shandwick House in Easter Ross which belonged to John Cockburn Ross, former owner of the lands we are now standing on. When the street was first built, only the south side (right as you face the West End), was called

Shandwick Place, the other side which was built at the same time was called Maitland Street.

Now an undistinguished part of the western development of the New Town, with much altered facades and shop fronts spoiling those which have been left intact, this was once the home of many famous figures. The most celebrated of these was Sir Walter Scott who lived at No. 6 Shandwick Place from 1827 until he retired as Clerk of the Session in 1830, and went to live permanently in Abbotsford. It was here that he wrote most of *Fair Maid of Perth, Anne of Geierstein,* and the second and third series of *Tales of a Grandfather.* In fact he wrote furiously here describing himself as 'a writing automaton'.

Across the road at No. 25 Maitland Street, lived Lockhart who became Scott's son-in-law and biographer, while 'Scott's close friend', Colin Mackenzie, lived down the street at No. 12 Shandwick Place. At No. 36 resided Patrick Fraser Tyler, renowned as the major and most accurate Scots historian of the first half of the 19th century.

On the left-hand side of the road is the massive Church of St George's West, designed by David Bryce, although its tower, whose height can best be appreciated from the other side of the road, was the work of Sir Rowand Anderson. The church was built as the Free Church of St George's in 1866–69 after the congregation's earlier church in Lothian Road had been demolished to make way for the new station. It was later called St George's West to distinguish it from St George's in Charlotte Square, now West Register House.

As you walk towards the West End notice the elaborate facades on some of the buildings such as those on the Maitland Hotel and the facing building. Reaching the junction of roads at the West End it is hard not to agree with a sad comment in the *Tatler,*

'Today the West End is more like the starting point for a motor rally than a meeting place in a civilised town.' In the hey-day of the New Town of course it presented a different and more elegant face.

If you wish to see the theatres and concert hall which are so vital to the Edinburgh Festival, turn right into Lothian Road. For the sake of dramatic effect, it would be pleasant to be able to say that, as the legend states, this road was built in a day. But alas there seems to be little foundation in the story that Sir John Clerk of Pennicuik bet a friend he would open a mile of road between daybreak and sunrise, adequate for him to drive his carriage through, and that he pressed unemployed men into service to perform this superhuman feat. In fact the road was made in the normal course of time in about 1787.

Walking up on the left we pass St Cuthbert's Church, the most recent of a succession of churches which have stood here since the 8th century. One of these was the church to which the villagers of Stockbridge and Dean Village used to trudge up through Kirkbraehead. The present church is actually late Victorian, being built in 1892, but the spire remains from the earlier church built in 1789. By the wall on this side is the old watchtower which was used to guard the newly dead from 'grave-snatchers'. Pass King's Stables Road, once an old jousting ground, and Castle Terrace built in the 19th century to provide a link with the Old Town, and you soon come to the Usher Hall on your left.

This hall is named after Andrew Usher, the head of an Edinburgh distilling family who in 1896 offered £100,000 to 'promote and extend the cultivation of, and taste for, music, not only in Edinburgh, but throughout the country'. Unfortunately due to the dilatory behaviour of the Corporation and much controversy about its site, the foundation stone of the hall was not laid until 1911, by which time Mr Usher was dead! However, his wish was fulfilled and the Usher Hall has become the chief concert hall in the city.

The hall itself is a large, squat building with a low green dome providing some relief from its dark stonework. The foundation stones laid by King George V and Queen Mary are to the left of the front, while on the front and round to the right in Grindlay Street, are several statues and carvings. These represent such things as 'the Soul of Music' and 'the Music of the Sea' and the two classical figures are of 'Musical Inspiration' and 'Musical Achievement'. Inside the buildings are statues of Andrew Usher and of Kathleen Ferrier who gave many memorable performances here in the Edinburgh Festivals of 1947–52.

Round the corner to the right in Grindlay Street is the Royal Lyceum Theatre built in 1863, whose architecture contrasts sharply with that of the adjoining Usher Hall. It has a fine exterior decorated with Corinthian columns and an equally impressive interior lined by cast iron galleries.

From here you can either continue along Grindlay Street, turn left into Cornwall Street and then left into Castle Terrace, or rejoin Lothian Road in order to see the site of the old basin of the Union Canal. This is situated on the right just past the cross-roads but is now unfortunately covered up by a cinema and the building called Lothian House. But as a reminder of the former character of the spot notice the inscription high up on the centre of the facade which reads, 'Here stood Port Hopetoun 1822–1922'. The frieze around the front depicts activities associated with the canal.

From here retrace your steps down Lothian Road, either all the way down or turn right into Grindlay Street and pick up the first route. Turn left into Castle Terrace and walk along with the sight of the Castle to your right. Towards the end of the road notice the attractive St John's Unitarian Church and shortly after this turn right and return to the West End.

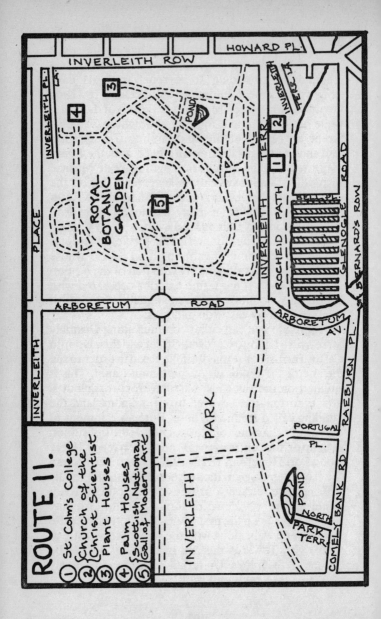

ROUTE 11.

1. St. Colm's College
2. Church of the Christ Scientist
3. Plant Houses
4. Palm Houses
5. Scottish National Gall. of Modern Art

INVERLEITH ROW
HOWARD PL.
INVERLEITH PL. LA.
INVERLEITH PLACE
INVERLEITH
ROYAL BOTANIC GARDEN
POND
INVERLEITH TERR.
INVERLEITH TERR. LA.
ROCHEID PATH
GLENOGLE ROAD
ST. BERNARD'S ROW
ARBORETUM ROAD
ARBORETUM AV.
INVERLEITH PARK
PORTUGAL PL.
COMELY BANK RD.
RAEBURN PL.
POND
NORTH PARK TERR.

Route 11

THE BOTANIC GARDEN AND INVERLEITH PARK

Edinburgh's Botanic Garden occupies a superb hilly site with magnificent views over the city. Its position combined with its wealth of lovely trees and flowers make the Garden a beautiful place for a walk. Indeed keen horticulturists or botanists may wish to omit the earlier section of the walk to concentrate on the Garden. In this case turn to page 106. Otherwise start your walk at the end of St Bernard's Row in Stockbridge.

Walk past the picturesque riverside cottages and cross the Water of Leith at Falshaw Bridge, originally opened in 1877, and bend round to the right to come into Glenogle Road. To the left of the road are the streets known as, 'the Colonies'. These were built in the 1860s by the Edinburgh Co-operative Building Society to provide model homes for working class people. They are in an attractive setting with the river at right angles to the terraces and if you look carefully you will find carvings on the Glenogle Road end of the rows. These depict the tools used to build the houses such as those of the carpenter or mason. After the Victorian swimming baths on the right the side of the road rises in a high bank.

Walk down the last terrace to the left, Bell Place, and cross the river on a wooden bridge. Turn right and walk along the river past new Barratt houses to the right. To your left are the impressive house and gardens of the Church of Scotland Missionary College, St Colm's, followed by the equally grand church of the Christian Scientists. Follow the path round and turn left into Inverleith Row.

After the rural flavour of the walk so far we come

out into a wide spacious road with some fine houses. Notice, for instance, the house on the corner of Inverleith Terrace whose elegant Corinthian pillars jut out over the road. To the right at No. 8 Howard Place, the author Robert Louis Stevenson was born in 1850. A path off to the left takes you into the Royal Botanic Garden.

You are now in the second oldest botanic garden in Britain, only the garden at Oxford is older. Although the Garden has only occupied its present site since the 1820s the first botanic garden in Edinburgh was founded in 1670 when two friends, Dr Robert Sibbald, the first Professor of Medicine at Edinburgh University, and Dr Andrew Balfour, who had studied in London, started to grow medical plants on a small piece of land 40 feet square, at St Anne's Yard near Holyrood Palace. In 1676 Balfour and Sibbald extended their activities to a garden belonging to Trinity Hospital, now the site of Waverley Station. This fact is recorded on a plaque on the wall of the station near platforms 10 and 11.

In 1761 the then Regius Keeper, John Hope, united the town and royal gardens which later moved to a site on the Leith Road. This proved to be a half-way stopping point for from 1820 onwards the gardens were moved to their present site. The operation was a mammoth task and accomplished with the aid of an ingenious transplanting machine invented by the overseer of this move, the horticulturalist William McNab. This machine allowed the moving of large mature trees from one spot to another, with the trees still miraculously remaining alive and well.

This walk takes you fairly briskly through the Garden and those who wish to spend more time here can buy a fully illustrated guide which gives a comprehensive tour of the Garden. For our walk, branch off to the left towards the Heath Garden which contains a large selection of heathers including 30 varieties of Scottish heather. From the Heath Garden we come to the pool and rocky slopes of the Rock Garden which was begun at the end of the 19th century, but was rebuilt between 1908 and 1914. Many Alpine plants are to be seen here while the rocks themselves are covered with herbaceous plants and creeping shrubs. The path takes us through to the Woodland Garden, full of conifers and rhododendrons, which are best seen in April and May when most of the rhododendrons are out in flower.

After the Woodland Garden take a right fork (the second you've come to) and then right again so you are doubling back on yourself. To your left is the Aboretum, the largest section of the Garden, and containing a wonderful variety of trees and shrubs from oaks, poplars and hawthorns to more exotic varieties such as Betula Jacquemontii, a white-barked birch from the Himalayas. To your right are the terraces of the Peat Garden displaying plants which flourish in cold, moist conditions.

Past the Peat Garden take the second left towards the Exhibition Plant Houses. On your way you pass the pond which has a functional as well as decorative purpose. Once a bog, it now provides the main source of water for the stream which runs through the rock garden and is also host to many marshy and acquatic plants such as water lilies. The beautiful trees surrounding the pond help to make this one of the most attractive parts of the Garden.

This path takes us past the Herbarium and Library, a reminder of another vital function of the Botanic Garden. It is a very important taxonomic centre identifying and classifying plants from all over the world, especially from South West China, Asia and the Himalayas. The Herbarium contains at least one and a half million plant specimens preserved for research, while the library has over 75,000 volumes making it one of the best botanical collections in the world.

If you have time it is well worth visiting the Exhibition Hall and the Plant Houses. The Exhibition Hall was opened in 1970 and is used to display features of plant and sometimes animal life to visitors. To the left of the Hall are the Exhibition Plant Houses opened in 1967 and their interlocking sections give a fascinating and exotic taste of plant life. Beautifully landscaped, these houses are a sheer joy to wander through to see cacti of all different descriptions, numerous different kinds of acquatic plants, tropical plants, ferns and orchids and many, many more. Behind these plant houses are the two palm houses. The bigger one built in 1858 at 70 feet 6 inches is the tallest greenhouse in Britain.

Retrace your steps and take the second right fork towards the National Gallery of Modern Art. As you walk up the slope you are already beginning to get fine views but if you turn to the left at the T junction and walk towards the City Viewpoint, thoughtfully provided benches, will allow you to enjoy a magnificent view over the city with the Castle in the centre. On the path up to the National Gallery a view indicator identifies the main points of interest.

Not content with providing a wealth of colourful plants and a panoramic view, the Garden also contains the Scottish National Gallery of Modern Art housed in the 18th century Inverleith House. As a taste of the treasures inside the Gallery look at the statues in front of the house, some of which are by Henry Moore and Epstein. The entrance to the Gallery is through an archway to the left of the house. Sadly for the visitor to the Botanic Garden the Gallery is due shortly to move to another venue.

From the Gallery take the path towards the West Gate from which you can either branch off right towards the Rhododendron Walk, particularly worth it in May and June when the majority of the rhododendron are flowering, or you can leave the Garden by the West Gate. From here you can either turn left and walk down Arboretum Road which eventually takes you back to St Bernard's Row. Or if you wish to walk a little further cross the road and enter Inverleith Park. You pass through grandiose gates topped by lions built in the 1890s in memory of Alison Hay Dunlop and given by J. C. Dunlop, an Edinburgh Councillor.

Walk down until you come to a crossroads of paths where Mr Dunlop is remembered for his generosity in giving the gates by a granite fountain in his honour. Turn left and walk down the path until you come to steps to the boating lake, Inverleith Pond. In the past the inhabitants of Stockbridge used to come and use the slopes above the pond as a drying and bleaching green, but now all the activity you are likely to see is people walking their dogs or controlling model boats in the water. Walk round the pond and then turn right to leave the park at Portugal Place. This takes you past the grounds of the Edinburgh Academicals Rugby Club who, under the name of Raeburn Place Academic Field, first began their long history on 17th May, 1854.

At the end of Portugal Place turn left into Raeburn Place, named after Sir Henry Raeburn, the portrait painter and one time owner of this land. Raeburn Place takes you back to the beginning of St Bernard's Row where the walk began.

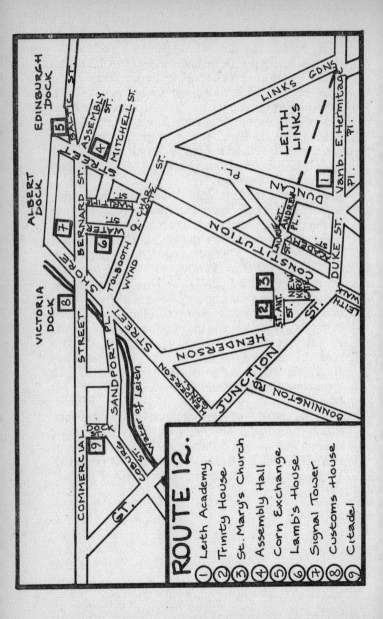

EDINBURGH DOCK
ALBERT DOCK
VICTORIA DOCK

BALTIC ST.
ASSEMBLY ST.
MITCHELL ST.
BERNARD STREET
WATER ST.
ST. MARTIN ST.
TOLBOOTH WYND
Q. CHARLOTTE ST.
SHORE
COMMERCIAL STREET
SANDPORT PL.
SANDPORT STREET
HENDERSON STREET
Water of Leith
COBURG ST.
GT. JUNCTION ST.
HENDERSON ST.
BONNINGTON RD.
JUNCTION RD.
ST. ANT.
ST. NEW KIRK GATE
LAURIE ST.
CONSTITUTION ST.
ST. ANDREW PL.
CADIZ ST.
DUKE ST.
LEITH WALK
DUNCAN PL.
LINKS GDNS
LINKS PL.
LEITH LINKS
Vanb. E. Hermitage Pl.

5
4
7
6
8
9
2
3
1

ROUTE 12.

① Leith Academy
② Trinity House
③ St. Mary's Church
④ Assembly Hall
⑤ Corn Exchange
⑥ Lamb's House
⑦ Signal Tower
⑧ Customs House
⑨ Citadel

110

Route 12

THE OLD PORT OF LEITH

This walk explores the town around the old port of Leith which was for centuries the chief gateway to Edinburgh. Nowadays no passengers land at Leith but the area has retained its own unique character.

One of the best ways to enter Leith is to take the path at the corner of James Place and East Hermitage Place which cuts across Leith Links. These links, now a park, formed one of the oldest golf courses in the world, being patronised in the past by such men as Charles I and the fiery preacher, John Knox. In 1642 they were the scene of what was possibly the first English versus Scottish golf championship. In this match, James, Duke of York and future King of England and Scotland, was partnered by an Edinburgh shoemaker, John Paterson, against two English lords. The Scottish side was victorious and from his share of the proceeds Paterson was able to build a splendid house, appropriately named, Golfer's Land, in the Canongate.

Whilst walking you pass two mounds, known as, Lady Fyfe's Brae and Giant's Brae, which were used to hold guns in the siege of Leith in 1560. According to legend Giant's Brae or Grave was the burial place of a herculean man, Ludovic Wilson, tyrannical overseer for the lairds of Leith. Wilson was killed on this spot by the Balfour family whose daughter he had once abducted.

At the end of the green continue along St Andrew Place noticing the classical building of St Andrew's Church which stands out from its undistinguished surrounds and is now unfortunately closed. Turn left into Academy Street and right to Duke Street where the glass roofs of the old Leith Central Station are visible above the tenements to the left.

We soon reach the crossroads and the entrance to old Leith. Although officially part of Edinburgh for much of its life, commercial and sea-faring Leith has a totally different atmosphere from professional Edinburgh, and its natives, 'Leithers' have a strong tradition of independence, and often hostility, towards Edinburgh. Officially amalgamated into Edinburgh in 1920, Leith is reputed to be the only part of Edinburgh Corporation where the locals talk about going 'to Edinburgh' rather than to 'the city centre'.

Passing the statue to Queen Victoria bearing a representation of her entry to Leith on September 3rd, 1842, walk straight through the new shopping centre to get to the old Kirkgate, the main street of old Leith. Once a maze of winding, narrow streets little remains of this part of town except for a few buildings such as the one on your left, Trinity House. This attractive sandy coloured building in classical style was built in 1816 on the site of a hospital opened for aged and poor seamen and their dependants in 1555. On the west wall, in St Anthony's Place (to the left) are two stones from the original hospital bearing the dates, 1555 and 1570.

Across the road is St Mary's Church or South Leith Parish Church whose life-story reflects the turbulent history of Leith. At various times the church served as a refuge – from the English invasion in 1544, as a prison, and as a store for ammunition in the Civil War. In 1848, the church underwent drastic reconstruction at the hands of Thomas Hamilton leaving very little of the original structure. The square tower replaced an earlier one destroyed in the wars of the sixteenth century whilst curiously the roof is supposed to be modelled on that of St Isaac's Church in Leningrad. The graveyard contains some very old graves, especially on the south side, and an unusual feature of arcades containing several famous graves, including those of the ancestors of Robert Louis Stevenson and Captain Gibson, leader of the disastrous Darien expedition sent to colonise part of Panama. The high walls around the graves were built to ward off eager body snatchers.

Retrace your steps back into the shopping centre and just past the huge anchor turn left and then left again into Constitution Street. Across the road in Laurie Street was once the house of the Oliphant family. Neighbours were woken early in the morning to find the debris of a collapsed house, and Mrs Oliphant dead in the rubble. The owner, barely alive, told how they had dreamed of buried treasure under this house and so had sold their possessions in Ayr and come to Leith to search. In their eager digging they had undermined the foundations of the house.

Constitution Street, part of the commercial quarter of 18th century Leith, contains some fine commercial and municipal buildings. Notice, for example, Nos. 121–5 on the right with stone fans over central pillars and enormous bow windows to the sides and centre. On the far corner of Queen Charlotte Street is the unusual building of the old Town Hall with a grand facade onto Constitution Street and a plainer one round the corner. Inbetween the Doric pillars on the Queen Charlotte Street side you will find the entrance to the police station.

To the right on Constitution Street is a curious stocky tower with a battlemented top, which is part of St John's Church, now in secular use. Although intended to be a, 'tall, slender spire', insufficient funds led to a compromise of an octagonal shape, whilst it has now lost the pinnacles on the top so looking even less slender! The Post Office on the corner of Mitchell Street is an attractive building with semicircular pediments over the windows and curious urn-like structures at the corners of the roof. In complete contrast notice the highly ornate, vividly painted, Nobles pub on the left.

On the corner of Constitution Street on the right is the long classical building which contains the Exchange Buildings and Assembly Rooms. These were built after part of the old fortifications of the port, which had been used by ladies for promenades, had been removed. A testament to grander days in Leith, the Assembly Rooms were completed in 1788 at a cost of £18,000 and once contained a ball room, coffee room, reading room and tavern. To the left the Exchange Buildings were built slightly later in 1809, and are now in commercial use.

At the end of the road cross over to look at the Corn Exchange on the corner of Baltic Street which is marked out by its distinctive green dome and octagonal tower. On the Constitution Street side notice the intricately carved stone frieze which shows the story of wheat from a mere seed to a loaf of bread. As you face the building bear left into Bernard Street and cross over the road past the statue to Burns in the centre.

Turn left into Bernard Street which also contains some impressive buildings. The finest of these, the domed building on the left was built in 1806 by the Leith Banking Company and then taken over by the National Bank of Scotland when the Leith Company failed in 1842. The building is a very harmonious structure with a classical facade and bowed front and central dome. The ceiling of the oval banking hall used to be painted with allegorical scenes until 70 years ago when they met with the disapproval of the then manager and were painted over at his orders.

Turn left into Carpet Lane leading to Water Street which takes you into the heart of industrial Leith full of old warehouses and factories with particularly splendid redbrick ones on the left. Sadly though, many of the warehouses here and elsewhere in Leith are empty and almost derelict, or else have completely disappeared. Continue on up Water Street until you come to the unusual Lamb's House on the right. Now an old people's day centre, this much restored 17th century house was once both the home and warehouse of a merchant. Notice the profusion of crow-stepped gables giving the house an almost geometrical design. It was in another earlier house on the same site that Mary, Queen of Scots stayed for an hour whilst Holyrood Palace was being prepared for her.

Looking up the road, blocks of flats line Tolbooth Wynd which on stormy nights was reputed to be haunted by a hearse-like vehicle with a headless driver and horse. The driver was supposed to be Miss Lucy Neville shot through the heart by Mr Fraser whilst trying to kidnap her, and so force her to be his bride. The coach carrying the dead girl hurtled down towards Tolbooth Wynd crushing Henry Tarbet, who tried to save Miss Neville, under its wheels.

Turn right into Burgess Street which brings you out to The Shore, which, true to its name, runs along the eastern side of the mouth of the Water of Leith. This is best seen at high tide when the swans and ducks on the water present a picturesque sight. The stone bridge on the left is on the site of the original bridge in Leith built in the 15th century.

Walking back towards Bernard Street the pub on the corner on the right, the King's Wark, marks the site of an older building of the same name. The first building was erected here in 1434 by James I as a Royal residence and was also used to house shipbuilding materials and stores for Holyrood Palace. Mainly destroyed during the Earl of Hertford's invasion in

1544, it was rebuilt by James VI in 1618. The King created the King's Wark and the adjacent lands and buildings a Barony and gave it into the care of Bernard Lindsay, groom of chambers. This charter empowered Lindsay to keep 4 taverns on the site, and granted him a tax of £4 for every tun of wine sold. Now, however, little is left of the original 17th century building although Bernard Street still bears the groom's name.

Crossing Bernard Street you come to the old Ship Hotel with a ship carved in the centre under the roof. As you walk along the quayside one can remember the famous travellers who disembarked at The Shore. In 1621, Mary, Queen of Scots, landed here after 13 years in France, on a day about which John Knox ominously remarked, 'never was seen so dolorous a face of heaven'. John Knox himself landed here from exile in 1559 whilst in 1822 George IV landed here on his visit to Edinburgh.

On the right now rather hemmed in by other buildings is the Signal Tower, a round stone building built in 1685 by Robert Mylne as a windmill. It is a mark of the changes that this part of Leith has undergone that in the 19th century the shore of the Forth went right up to the tower. During the Napoleonic Wars the tower was adapted to signal the state of the tide and depth of the water at the harbour bar to the ships in the estuary. The windows and battlemented top were added later.

Across the water a collection of old ironwork and bollards, together with the original iron bridge, form the remains of the old Leith Docks, built at the beginning of the 19th century by the engineer, John Rennie. These are now filled in and new docks, Imperial, Victoria, Albert and Edinburgh Docks were built between 1852 and 1881 after over 80 acres of land had been reclaimed from the estuary.

Retrace your steps to Bernard Street and cross the bridge to Commercial Street. Just across the water on the right is the imposing Customs House, best appreciated from the opposite side of the road. Gaining stature because of the space around it, this building was designed by Robert Reid in 1812 in a Greek Doric style with a large pediment containing the Royal Crest of a lion and unicorn. The rest of Commercial Street mainly contains large bonded warehouses such as Macdonald and Muir.

Take the second left turning into Dock Street where on the right you can see the remains of the old Citadel. This was built in the Civil War to house Cromwell's troops in return for the confirmation of the City Council's rights and privileges. Largely destroyed on the Restoration and the accession of Charles II to the throne in 1660, all that now remains is the arch which formed the entrance to the fort.

Turning right into Coburg Street you pass along the side of the north Leith burial ground, in existence since the 18th century, while on the corner of Couper Street on the right are the grand premises of Melrose Ltd., Tea Merchants. Before leaving Coburg Street look back down the river for a fine view of industrial Leith and its old warehouses. You may like to take the path by the river which runs along a disused railway track to Warriston Crescent at Canonmills from where you can cut through the New Town to Princes Street. On your way you pass the remains of Bonnington Mill and Warriston burial ground. But for this route turn left and cross the river again.

Great Junction Street, which takes you back to the foot of Leith Walk, roughly follows the old Leith boundary line. Mainly consisting of shops there are some interesting buildings, such as the Edwardian premises of the Leith Provident Co-operative on the left on the corner of Taylor Gardens. Further down on the left are the huge offices of John Crabbie & Company, famous for their green ginger wine, often taken with whisky. On the right, Great Junction Street Public School was once Robert Bell's school, established in 1838, where he pioneered his monitorial system of education. This worked by teaching lessons by rote to monitors who then repeated the lessons to their classmates thus economising on the teacher's time.

Shortly after this you emerge at the foot of Leith Walk, the end of this walk.

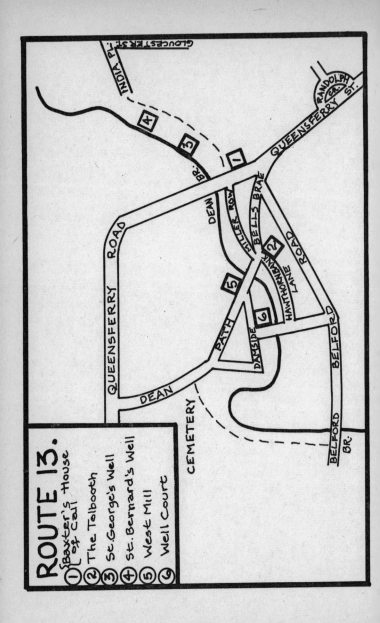

ROUTE 13.
1. Baxter's House & Gaol
2. The Talbooth
3. St.George's Well
4. St. Bernard's Well
5. West Mill
6. Well Court

GLOUCESTER ST.
INDIA PL.
RANDOLPH CR.
QUEENSFERRY ST.
DEAN BR.
BELLS BRAE
MILLER ROW
DEAN ROAD
QUEENSFERRY ROAD
DEAN PATH
DAMSIDE
HAWTHORNBANK LANE
BELFORD ROAD
BELFORD BR.
DEAN
CEMETERY

120

Route 13

DEAN VILLAGE

This walk explores Dean Village, a delightful riverside spot just five minutes from the city centre.

Walk down Queensferry Street and stop just as you reach the massive Dean Bridge and look at the house edging onto the bridge. This building, once called the Baxter's House of Call, was the old village inn. If you walk round to the north-east wall (facing onto the bridge), an emblem over the gate will give you some idea of the kind of community it served. The stone carving that you can see is the Baker's Stone from 1619 and shows wheatsheaves, the sun and baker's shovels together with a quotation from Genesis, 'In the sweat of thy face shalt thou eat bread'. From this stone, taken from an old mill, you will gather that the customers of this inn were millers from the village, straddling the Water of Leith below, and which by the 17th century was operating as many as 11 water mills.

The village was originally called the Village of the Water of Leith, although it was recorded in a 12th century charter as the Mills at the Dene. Now known as Dean Village, this community once provided all the flour for Edinburgh and the villages round about. Nowadays Dean Village is a sought after residential centre but there are still remnants from its milling days which we will visit on our walk.

Turn left just before the bridge and walk down the steep slope of Bell's Brae. Despite its severe gradient this was once the main road out to the Queen's ferry and the north. As you walk down the road you can see buildings which formerly served as stables (to the left) and as coachhouses (to the right). The coachhouses, now used by a firm of architects, were in use as late as

1900. If you can imagine it the coaches used to do the journey to the Queen's ferry, some 10 miles, in forty minutes.

At the bottom of the hill you come to the large grey building which was once the hub of the milling village. This was the Tolbooth which both housed the H.Q. of the baker's trade union called the Incorporation of Baxters, and served as their granary. Although in some respects its external appearance looks quite modern, details such as the cut-away corners and arches over the windows, suggest the building's true age. The Tolbooth was in fact erected in 1675 when the village was firmly established as a milling centre.

To the right of the building are several inscriptions from which you can just make out the words, 'God's Providence is our Inheritance' and 'God bless the Baxters of Edinburgh who built this house'. Some of the words are difficult to decipher but those which are clear demonstrate the occupation followed by the first owners of this building.

In the 12th century the rights of the profits of the flour mills were conferred on the canons of Holyrood Abbey; these rights were later inherited by the Incorporation of Baxters. This in turn led to the ceremony of the 'feuing of the millers'. Each spring the bakers walked in procession down to the village to settle prices and wages for the next year, and then celebrated at a local inn, in all probability the Baxter's House of Call, which we have just visited. Suitably replenished, and the records indicate they did not stint themselves in their celebrations, the millers returned to the city.

Now, unfortunately this procession is just a memory. No milling takes place in the village anymore, and most of the mills are just remembered by a few relics from the old buildings. There is one of these opposite the Tolbooth by the bridge in the form of a stone carved with the inscription of 'Blessed be God for all His Gifts', which came from Lindsay's Mill which has now disappeared.

Miller Row to the right is another reminder of the old character of the village and we will explore it later. Now turn up left into Hawthornbank Lane by the Tolbooth. On the right just as you enter the lane is another 17th century house. Further up on the left is an attractive row of cottages with wooden beams and colour-washed stone which were renovated in 1981. From here you have a fine view over the buildings in Damside. To explore these in more detail cross the river by the wooden bridge which is situated by the side of the ancient ford. On the left used to stand the tannery buildings and the land is now due for rede-velopment. With the decline of most of its industry, such as the milling, weaving as well as tannery trades, much of the village fell into disrepair. Many buildings have now been restored but in 1981 there is still a lot to be done.

Damside used to be lined by weavers' cottages but by the 19th century they too were in a bad state of repair. The proprietor of *The Scotsman*, John Ritchie Findlay, paid for the cottages to be pulled down and an entirely new development, Well Court, to be erected in their place. Mr Findlay may have had some practical reasons for his generosity for the squalor of the old cottages was spoiling the view from his home which overlooked the village. The buildings were designed by Sydney Mitchell and with their interest-ing roof lines, gables and a large tower in the far left hand corner they make a contrast, if a pleasing one, with the rest of the village. It is thought possible that the plan of Well Court may have been influenced by the ideas of Patrick Geddes, a great pioneer in social and housing matters.

As you reach the village again you can see the Victorian school on the right. Turn left into Dean Path which used to be the route out of the village for the coaches. This street is a mixture of houses which have already been reconstructed, like those at the bottom of the hill, and those still awaiting renovation.

At the top of Dean Path used to be the original Dean Village which housed the quarry workers from Craigleith and the workers from the estate of Dean House. This was situated where the cemetery now is and almost nothing remains of the original settlement, even its name has been transferred to the original Water of Leith Village. If you wish to investigate the cemetery you will find there the graves of several famous men, including Lord Cockburn, who apart from being a notable judge was a prolific and much quoted commentator on the Edinburgh of Sir Walter Scott. William Playfair, responsible for so many of the city's classical buildings such as the two art galleries on the Mound and Surgeon's Hall, is also buried here.

But if instead of continuing up the path, you turn left by a signpost pointing to Belford Bridge, winding steps will lead you down to the river again. Turn right and a quiet, if at times a little muddy, path takes you along by the river bank, and eventually brings you out at Belford Bridge. Just before you climb the steps notice the two unicorns supporting the city Coat of Arms on the wall. Climb the steps to the bridge and cross the water. Belford Bridge replaces another earlier bridge and nearby used to be a small hamlet, built around Bell's Mill. The mill has now been destroyed in a fire, but its granary has been incorporated into the new Dragonara Hotel, and the miller's house also survives.

Walk along Belford Road a little way and turn left just past the post office and back down into Hawthornbank Lane again to enjoy another very fine walk by the river. This begins at Miller Row at the foot of Bell's Brae.

But before going down the road look across the river to the left where the bank is dominated by West Mill, the only mill left surviving intact in the village. If you look at the bottom of the mill on the wall facing you you can see the twin arches of the tail-race. The circular openings above, now blocked up, once allowed ventilation onto the grain. The mill is now converted into luxury flats with wonderful views over the river.

Turn right down into Miller Row which was once a busy thoroughfare between several mills, Jericho and Lindsay's Mills, and further down, Mar's Mill. As you walk down the path you can hear the river, now relatively tranquil, but once the motor of a thriving community. By the river are three Normandy grind-stones marking the site of Lindsay's Mill.

The magnificent arches of Dean Bridge are now well in view. This was designed by Thomas Telford, virtually the last thing he did before his death, erected in 1832 and built to a height of 108 feet above the water. Noticing a small building just this side of the bridge which was once Mar's Mill, pass under the bridge. It is difficult not to feel dwarfed by this feat of engineering and extraordinary to recollect that this bridge was built at the whim of a private individual, who also picked up most of the bill, so access could be provided to a new development he was planning across the river. Nowadays Dean Bridge provides the main route to the north, usurping the role of Dean Village and its bridge which once performed this vital function.

Leave the village behind and walk along a path by the river which is now deep in a gorge. Indeed this is how the village acquired its current name for Dean means gorge. You soon pass a small building to your left with the date 1810 on it. This is St George's Well but dwarfing it in size and grandeur is the second well on the river, a little further down. As you approach this building the site of a statue under a dome does not immediately put you in mind of a well. The well is in fact modelled on a classical temple and the woman in the centre represents Hygeia, the Goddess of Health. Walk down the steps to have a closer look at it.

St Bernard's Well has its origins in a tale concerning the missionary, Saint Bernard. Hearing that Scotland was a country 'rich in faith' he visited it. Unfortunately he did not find the locals as receptive or as friendly as he had hoped, and so dispirited and ill he retreated to a cave near a spring by this river. Miraculously his health was restored and he ascribed this recovery to the healing waters of the spring and the beauty of the scenery, and so it is said St Bernard's Well was founded. In fact there are no records of St Bernard ever having visited Scotland although there are those who say they played in St Bernard's cave near here in their youth.

The well was neglected in the Reformation which was not over-enthusiastic about saints and then rediscovered in the 1780s. The well was bought by Lord Gardenstone who commissioned Alexander Nasmyth to design a temple for it on the lines of a temple in Tivoli, Italy. The present statue replaced an earlier one in the 19th century. The well quickly became very fashionable and rules were drawn up governing its use. It was to cost 1d for adults, ½d for children, and drinkers were supposed to walk around for five minutes after drinking, 'both as a benefit to themselves, and to make way for other water drinkers'. In 1790 a book was published entitled, *A Medical Treatise on the Virtues of St Bernard's Well, Illustrated with Severe Cases*. According to this treatise the taste of the waters was 'at first unpalatable but from use becoming pleasant and agreeable'.

In the 19th century the well fell into neglect once more until William Nelson the publisher, who was so impressed with the power of the sulphurous waters that he used to walk three miles every day to drink them, bought the well. He refurbished it and the grounds and installed the new statue of Hygeia. Mr Nelson is remembered for his generosity by a plaque to the right of the well. Up till the 1950s it was possible to drink from the well. Now it is shut up but there is a pleasant riverside walk for a little way until the sudden noise of traffic tells you cars are passing overhead.

Climb the steps which take you into Stockbridge. From here you can turn right and then left into India Place and then turn up right into Gloucester Street which takes you back to the city centre.

ROUTE 14.

① Surgeon's Hall
② Old College
③ Royal Scottish Mus.
④ Greyfriars Church
⑤ George Heriot's Sch.
⑥ Student Centre
⑦ Appleton Tower
⑧ David Hume Tower
⑨ Library
⑩ McEwan Hall
⑪ Medical School
⑫ Royal Infirmary

Route 14

THE UNIVERSITY AND GREYFRIARS BOBBY

This walk explores the area around Edinburgh University, the 6th oldest university in Britain.

Begin the walk at the junction of the High Street with the top of South Bridge. This bridge was built in 1786–88 and its 19 arches span the Cowgate running far below. Walk down the gentle slope away from the town until you come to Chambers Street and the imposing domed building on the right. We will examine this more closely shortly but first continue up Nicolson Street a little way until you come to a huge classically styled building on the left which is the Surgeon's Hall.

Surgeons began life in tandem with barbers – the connection is obvious if a little disconcerting. After the church decided that their healing work was interfering with their spiritual work, minor operations were entrusted to these two sets of people. Gradually the barbers were eased out of this partnership and in 1788 the surgeons were incorporated as the Royal College of Surgeons. In 1833 a new hall was built by William Playfair to match their new status. Their old hall still stands, although now somewhat altered, in Drummond Street nearby.

As you stand in the hectic Nicolson Street it is difficult to believe that this once led through a large park surrounding Nicolson House. If you turn and face South Bridge and the way you have come, you can see that the road slopes down towards Chambers Street and then more steeply upwards. This was no accident but was caused by the personal whim of Robert Dundas, Lord President of the Court of

Session. In the 18th century he had a house in Adam Square which is now the east part of Chambers Street which looks onto South Bridge. If the bridge had been built on the level with no dip in it as would have been logical, Robert Dundas's house would have been under the level of the new bridge. Since one of the commissioners in charge of the bridge's construction was Dundas's half-brother, they agreed to slope the bridge down to the present Chambers Street so the entrance of the house was at street level. Ironically Dundas died in 1787, a year before the bridge was opened.

Walk back towards Chambers Street and look to your right down Infirmary Street. It was here, at the top of Robertson Close, that the Royal Infirmary of Edinburgh had its humble beginnings in 1729. It was also here at the bottom of the street that the young Walter Scott was educated at the High School. The institution also taught Lord Cockburn, a memorable commentator on the Edinburgh scene. In the 1820s it was decided that the school was too small and inconvenient for the population, many of whom had moved to the New Town, and a grand new school was built on Calton Hill.

The corner of Chambers Street and South Bridge is filled, and dominated, by Old College, the finest of the University buildings. As the inscription above the entrance tells you, Edinburgh University can be said to have begun about 1582, although it actually started teaching in 1583. Originally called the Tounis College, i.e. belonging to the town, it was established in accordance with the ethics of the Protestant Reformation to produce good men who would also be intelligent and responsible citizens. A charter of James VI authorised the establishment of the College and ordered that it be called King James College which is how it is labelled, although in fact it was rarely called this.

The original site of the University, roughly the same as the one facing you, was the Kirk o' Fields, where Lord Darnley, the second husband of Mary, Queen of Scots, perished in the explosion of a house on the site in 1557. By the 18th century the buildings were getting very dilapidated, being described by one American visitor as, 'a most miserable musty pile scarce fit for stables'. The famous architect Robert Adam drew up designs for a grand new building; subscriptions were obtained from the public and the foundation stone was laid in 1789. There was much excitement in the air expressed by the foundation procession who sang the following verse:

The stone we've seen first placed by Napier's hand,
Whose future pile aloft shall rise,
Whose fame shall spread through every distant land,
And raised by time, shall reach the skies.

In 1792 Adam died leaving behind a half-finished building and plans for the rest of the College which the outbreak of war with France, in 1793, effectively stifled. There was now little money for, or interest in, the enterprise. Eventually at the end of the war Parliament granted £10,000 for several years to finish the building, which was eventually completed by the architect William Playfair.

But as we enter through the massive entrance underneath the Doric pillars, each of which is a mono-lith, i.e. fashioned from a single block of stone, we enter under a part built according to Adam's own design. As we look around the courtyard much is also how Adam envisaged it with the major difference that there is only one courtyard and not two as originally planned.

As we look back towards the entrance and the huge dome we see another deviation from the original design. This was added later by Rowand Anderson in 1887. Above it is a gilded statue representing a 'Youth holding aloft the torch of knowledge'. The layout of the quadrangle is roughly symmetrical with its four sweeping staircases on the north and south sides, and curved colonnaded pieces linking the blocks at the corner. In the far left-hand corner (south-west) is the Talbot Rice Art Centre while along the south side is Playfair's Upper Library, once the main University library and considered to be one of the finest examples of classical design anywhere in Britain.

Having walked round the courtyard leave Old College and turn left and then left again into Chambers Street. On your left is the back of Old College while the newer building opposite is Adam House, built in 1935 as an examination hall for the University. For a 20th century building it has an unusual arched facade which fits in well with the older creation of Robert Adam opposite. The exam rooms were built at the back of the building away from the noise of the traffic.

Cross the road and a couple of yards on the right down Guthrie Street is a small plaque marking the site of the house where Walter Scott was born. The house itself is long gone.

Across the road is the long building of the Royal Scottish Museum. Under the name, the Industrial Museum of Scotland, this was founded in 1854 and the present building which dates from 1861, was designed by Captain Fowkes. It has quite an attractive facade in the Venetian Renaissance style with arched windows adding a touch of elegance. But its heavy exterior appearance is in complete contrast with the beautiful interior composed of cast iron galleries under a glass roof. It is said to have been influenced by the design of Crystal Palace and the modern addition of pools and greenery only serves to enhance its light and airy qualities. The museum itself is the largest general museum in Europe and contains an enormous variety of exhibits from steam engines to stuffed animals and Egyptian relics to rock samples. Particularly impressive is the skeleton of a blue whale suspended over a gallery. The whale, 78 feet long, was stranded at North Berwick in 1832.

Opposite the Gallery is a statue of William Chambers who as Lord Provost of Edinburgh from 1865–69 was active in the concern over the city's public health which eventually led to slum clearances, of which this street was one product.

On the other side of the road is one of the buildings of Edinburgh's newer university, Heriot Watt. This started life as the School of Arts and Mechanics Institute in 1821 and was later renamed the Watt Institution in honour of the engineer, James Watt, a statue of whom stands outside the building. After amalgamating its endowments with those of the George Heriot Hospital it became the Heriot Watt College, finally to become the Heriot Watt University in 1965. Now most of its buildings are on a separate campus on the edge of the city at Riccarton, but this building still houses the library and some other departments.

Leave Chambers Street and cross the road to the small statue of a dog at the top of Candlemaker Row. This dog was no ordinary dog but became the subject of many tales and a Walt Disney Film. This was Bobby, a small Skye terrier (although that did not prevent Holywood casting him as a collie) who kept faithful vigil on the grave of his master, John Gray, for 14 years in the Greyfriars churchyard nearby. One day Bobby was arrested as a vagrant but such was the public interest in this small dog that William Chambers, as Lord Provost, paid his licence that year and all subsequent years, and even gave him a collar with the inscription, 'Greyfriars Bobby, from the Lord Provost 1867, Licensed'. The fountain topped by the figure of the dog was given by Baroness Burdett Coutts but it is no longer in working order.

Greyfriars Church and graveyard, which lie back from the road behind the fountain, have a memorable history. The church was built on the site of an old friary, hence its name, and has had a chequered life. In 1620 a new church was built, and then in 1718 the tower, which had been storing gunpowder, blew up and damaged much of the church. The old part was walled up and a new church was built in 1772. In 1845 fire again struck and the church was reconstructed. In 1938 the wall dividing the two churches was knocked down leaving one large church.

The churchyard is older than the church, being built in the 16th century to remove the pressure on St Giles' graveyard. It contains the graves of some of the city's most famous men including Henry Mackenzie, author of *The Man of Feeling;* Allan Ramsay the wigmaker turned poet; the architect William Adam; James Hutton, seen as the 'Father of Modern Geology'; and Joseph Black, the inventor of the theory of latent heat. It was also here that the National Covenant, declaring the unity of the Scottish people and their determination to uphold the Reformed i.e. Presbyterian, tradition, was signed on a tombstone in 1638. This was the beginning of a bitter warfare with the English King and his attempts to impose bishops and an Episcopalian Church of Scotland.

If you walk to the far left-hand side of the graveyard you will find the enclosure of the Covenanters Prison. Here during the winter of 1679, nearly

1,200 prisoners were imprisoned at the mercy of the elements. Not surprisingly many died of exposure; those who did survive were either hanged in the Grassmarket or sent off to America, although the ship taking them there capsized off the Orkneys and many drowned. A memorial to the Covenanters is situated on the other side of the churchyard which also contains the grave of John Gray and his faithful dog Bobby, who was buried there on the orders of Queen Victoria.

Slightly to the right of the Covenanters Prison a gate leads on to the magnificent George Heriot's Hospital or School. This owes its foundation to the generosity of George Heriot, a jeweller who amassed a considerable fortune lending to James VI and his Court. Nicknamed 'Jinglin' Geordie' he left £23,000 on his death in 1624 for the 'maintenance, relief and bringing up' of poor and fatherless boys. The present building was begun in 1628 but was then comandeered by Cromwell in the Civil War. Eventually in 1659, 30 boys were admitted; later in 1886 the school was turned into a fee-paying school with 150 free places for fatherless boys. The school with its distinctive corner towers and smaller octagonal ones has justly been described as 'the most complete embodiment of the Jacobean conception of formal architecture in the whole of Scotland'.

Leave the churchyard and take the second right fork into Bristo Place, and then cross over the dual carriageway into Bristo Square, a new square created by the University in 1981. Walk towards the tall towers of George Square, past a few old houses and then you are face to face with the new complex of University buildings.

George Square is almost completely changed from its original character. When it was built in 1766 it was the most exclusive development in the city, the first expansion of the wealthy out of the over-crowded Old Town. It was a speculative venture on the part of James Brown who named the square after his brother, and not after the King as might be supposed. The title deeds of the first properties forbade 'brewing or baking . . . participation in any handicraft . . . and dealing in or the occupation of any Trade or Merchandise'. The earliest residents were of the highest social class and included Henry Dundas, Viscount Melville; Sir Ralph Abercromby; Robert Macqueen, Lord Brafield, the so-called 'hanging judge' and the prototype for Robert Louis Stevenson's *Weir of Hermiston;* and also Walter Scott, senior. Shortly after the birth of young Scott the author, his father moved his family to George Square and it was here that Scott stayed until his marriage in 1797.

Gradually the square began to acquire educational institutions and by the 20th century the University had begun to buy up much of the square for its own purposes. The stage was thus set for the 'Battle of George Square', involving the University versus the conservationists over the University's plans to build a large new complex of buildings, and demolish the existing houses. Eventually the University won and although the west side was left intact this concession did little to salve the wounds of the opposition. The programme went rapidly ahead and by 1962 the tall arts tower, called the David Hume Tower after the enlightenment philosopher, was erected.

Other buildings followed thick and fast including the William Robertson Building named after a renowned historian who was Principal of the University at the time of the erection of Old College. Behind this is the Appleton Tower, the tallest and one of the least successful buildings in the complex at 173 feet tall, providing rather an eyesore on the Edinburgh skyline. Indeed the critics of the George Square buildings have not been slow to point out that the tower is a fitting monument to the man, who as Principal, was responsible for the promotion of the new development, and after whom the tower was named.

Round the corner is the Adam Ferguson building while the south side is completed by the long low library building, designed by Sir Basil Spence, the architect of Coventry Cathedral. This was completed in 1967 to house two million books and has been widely praised for the way its 'strong and effective lines' tone in well with the rest of the square.

But when we come round to the west side of the square and see the way the remaining houses have been swamped by the giant University buildings it is hard to feel enthusiastic about the architecture of the complex, whatever its intrinsic merits. This is particularly so when the surviving houses give a tantalising idea of what the square must once have looked like. The first house in the row, No. 29, was owned by James Brown who built the square, while a little further along, No. 25 was the home of the Scott family.

The last side of the square is devoted to medical science buildings such as the bio-chemistry, pharmacology and psychology departments. On the corner of the square is the Student's Union opened in 1889, and then you pass by the multi-sided McEwan Hall, a gift to the University in 1897 from the McEwan & Co. brewing firm, which now houses large gatherings such as the Graduation ceremonies.

Just past this turn left into the Medical School. Edinburgh quickly developed and retained a reputation for medicine and in 1883 this new building was opened. Here, according to the University's historian, Sir Alexander Grant, 'all that is repulsive in the study of Medicine is mitigated and refined'. As you go into the courtyard, on your right is a memorial to the Polish School of Medicine which was established here in the last war when Poland was occupied by the Nazis. On the other side Robert Lind, the conqueror of scurvy, is remembered by a plaque. Further down on the left is another memorial, this time from the McGill University in memory of the four founders of their Faculty of Medicine who were trained in Edinburgh. A door off to the left gives access onto the McEwan Hall.

Leave the quad and cross the road into Forrest Road. Look across the road to see the enormous mass of buildings making up the Royal Infirmary. This is the third incarnation of the Royal Infirmary: the second building, completed by 1748, became too small for the teaching and medical demands which it faced, and so in 1870, the foundation stone was laid for the present building. Originally having 555 beds, it has grown dramatically and now comprises a complete complex of maternity, eye, haematology, accident and emergency departments etc. Once again it has outgrown itself and an extension is now being built.

Forrest Road takes you back to George IV Bridge and the end of the walk.

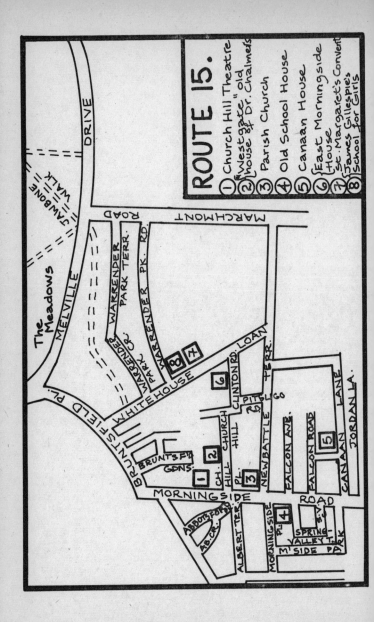

ROUTE 15.

1. Church Hill Theatre
2. "Westgate" old House of Dr. Chalmers
3. Parish Church
4. Old School House
5. Canaan House
6. East Morningside House
7. St. Margaret's Convent
8. James Gillespie's School for Girls

Route 15

THE MEADOWS AND MORNINGSIDE

This walk begins at the northern end of Jawbone Walk as it branches off right from Middle Meadow Walk. Were you walking down this path in the 1500s you would have had exceedingly wet feet for this area, now known as, 'the Meadows', was once the South Loch, the town's main supply of drinking water. By the 17th century the loch, which was also used by the brewers situated on its shores, had shrunk considerably and in 1621 it was decided to drain the loch.

Jawbone Walk is particularly beautiful in late Spring when all the cherry trees, which line the path, are out in bloom. The source for the path's curious name is found in the arches at the southern end which were once a whale's jaw. This was donated by the Zetland and Fair Isle knitting stand when an International Exhibition was held on the Meadows in 1886.

Cross Melville Drive, the old southern boundary of the loch, and turn right into a path parallel to the road. Bruntsfield Links, to the right, which claims to be the city's oldest municipal golf course, is one of the few open parts remaining of the old Burgh Muir or Moor. The rest disappeared long ago being replaced by settlements such as those at Morningside. The path takes you past Warrender Park Crescent named after the Warrender family, once lairds of the Bruntsfield Estate.

Continue along the path on the other side of the road noting the fine houses which are now visible on Bruntsfield Place to the right. One in particular is especially pleasing with its harmonious proportions highlighted by the fanlight over the door and curving steps leading up to the entrance. As you leave the path and join the main road tall tenements take the place of open land. In plain style these flats are enlivened only by stone tracery on a few blocks such as those at Nos. 160–172 on the right.

On the left hand corner of Bruntsfield Place and Bruntsfield Gardens, a plaque at ground floor level represents an elegant house. This depicts the mansion of Greenhill which gives its name to many streets in the area. Demolished in 1844, stone from quarries in the grounds was used to build Bruntsfield Place.

As Bruntsfield Place turns into Morningside Road we come to the corner known as 'Holy Corner', because of the four churches to be found there. Most curious of these is Christ Church on the right with its tall spire and unusual semi-circular sanctuary. The tenement flats give way to pleasant two storey houses on the left as we climb the gentle slope towards Church Hill Theatre. Built in 1894 as the area's third Free Church, it was converted into a well equipped theatre in 1965. The first play to be performed there was *The Importance of Being Ernest* by Oscar Wilde and now the theatre is the chief venue for amateur drama in the city. Sticking out from its surroundings because of its red sandstone it is a heavily built, rather ugly building, with Ionic pillars on the first floor.

You are now on the summit of the old Burgh Muir and, although the area is now heavily developed, there are still fine views of the Pentland Hills. Turn left into Church Hill Place and stop at the first house on the left as Church Hill Place becomes Church Hill. No. 1 Church Hill, now called 'Westgate', was once known as 'Kirkhill' from which the area gets its name – Church Hill.

Kirkhill was the home of the famous church reformer, Dr Thomas Chalmers, who played a leading part in the 'Disruption' in 1843, when 470 ministers left the General Assembly of the Church of Scotland as a protest against state interference with the appointment of ministers. No longer able to use the established church, the new Free Church first met in Dr Chalmers's house with the congregation dispersed throughout the house – upstairs, downstairs and on the stairs. Through the gates we can see a gracious house and it is touching to recall Chalmers' slight sense of guilt at the pleasantness of his surroundings, 'mean to build at Morningside, but let me not forget the end of the world and the coming of Christ'.

Return to Morningside Road and across the road on the corner of Albert Terrace are the crow-stepped gables of Bank House, an 18th century house and the childhood home of Cosmo Gordon Lang, Archbishop of Canterbury from 1928–1942.

There is a flavour of Sir Walter Scott in the name of Abbotsford Park and Crescent named after the author's house. Before 1866 and the creation of one long Morningside Road, the flavour would have been even stronger: the section from the Baptist Church to Church Hill was known as 'Waverley Terrace' whilst its continuation to Abbotsford Park was called, 'Marmion' after Scott's famous poem.

The clue for these names is found in the legend of the Bore Stone which is situated on the left wall of the parish church. In a tradition established by Sir Walter Scott and described in his poem, *Marmion,* it was in this large, irregularly shaped stone that the Royal Standard was last pitched for the muster of the Scottish Army on Burgh Muir, before the disastrous Battle of Flodden. The plaque under the stone describes the tradition and recites some lines from *Marmion*. Unfortunately for this romantic idea it was discovered in 1942 that the stone contained nothing in which a standard's staff could have been put and that in fact the Royal Standard was never even hoisted on the Burgh Muir before Flodden, due to the simple fact it was still being made. The parish church, itself, built in 1834, is quite plain except for a central steeple clock.

The first villas built in the area in the 1820s were in Morningside Place to the right, originally called Deuchar Street, after the family who owned nearby Morningside House and surrounding lands. No. 6 was the home of the Misses Balfours, aunts of the young Robert Louis Stevenson, whose initials carved on a cupboard door mark his frequent childhood visits.

Morningside Place leads to Tipperlinn Road which leads to the Royal Edinburgh Hospital. This was built on the site of the old village of Tipperlinn, a weaving village, which disappeared as the new hospital grew in the 19th century.

Back on Morningside Road the curious squat building on the right is the Old Schoolhouse built in 1823. After the school closed in 1892 the mechanism of the clock was given to South Morningside Church, and so the school clock was for many years permanently stopped at twenty to four. Now, however, it is keeping time again and the building is used for religious purposes.

Just past Springvalley Terrace at No. 160 are two of the original two storey houses, and if you go down the alleyway or pend you will find one house which still has its old outside stone staircase.

Once you reach the ugly new pub, the Merlin, and the more attractive Edwardian Public Library you are in the heart of the old Morningside Village. It is hard to imagine the scene in 1850, described by James Grant in *Old and New Edinburgh* when Morningside as 'a row of thatched cottages, a line of trees and a blacksmith's forge still slumbered in rural solitude'. Established as an individual village by the 18th century, it became an important stopping point for farmers on the way to Edinburgh but it was the coming of the railway in 1872 which transformed Morningside from a village to a residential suburb of Edinburgh. Wealthy citizens rushed to build villas in this sunny or 'morningside' southern part of the city. It is perhaps from these people that Morningside gained its reputation for almost absurd respectability whose inhabitants were supposed to speak as if their mouths were full of silver marbles.

Running from Springvalley Gardens to the supermarket at the corner of Morningside Park were once the grounds of Morningside House. Thought to have been built in the second half of the 18th century, the house was destroyed in 1895. A plaque on the wall of the bank, once the house's front garden, commemorates the Diamond Jubilee of Queen Victoria. When it was in existence Morningside House was home to the eccentric Lord Gardenstone who was noted as a great lover of pigs, to the extent that he even used one to heat his bed as a hot water bottle!

At the entrance to Jordan Lane further down on the left, are the first tenement blocks built in Morningside in 1857. On the right-hand side of the road beyond the tenements are some of the original cottages, one of which, Ainslie Cottage, is said to have been the one-time residence of George Meikle Kemp, the architect of the Scott Monument.

Jordan Lane is only one of the biblical sounding streets in this area for parallel to it on the south is Nile Grove while to the north is Canaan Lane. Several theories have been advanced for the derivation of these names. Some say that the lands were named after a band of gypsies, claiming to be exiled Egyptians. Perhaps more plausibly, but less romantically, these streets may be named after Egypt Farm nearby.

Returning to Morningside Road, walk up it and turn right into Canaan Lane by the extravagantly decorated pub, the Canny Man's, whose many plaques on the wall bear little relation to the history of the pub. The real Canny Man is supposed to have been Mr James Kerr who owned a pub here and was supposed to have had a restraining effect on his customers, advising them to drink slowly and, 'ca' canny man'. To the right, the area between Canaan Lane and Jordan Lane was once known as 'Paradise' and its inhabitants, 'Paradisers', formed a small community of their own.

Canaan Lane still retains the quiet rural air which once characterised much of Morningside. *Blackwoods Magazine* described Canaan in 1821 as, 'grounds to the south of the city where a number of snug boxes attest to the taste of the inhabitants for country retirement and the pleasures of rustication'. These 'snug boxes' were actually palatial houses such as Canaan Lodge on the left, opposite the entrance to Woodburn Terrace. This house set well back in its grounds once housed Professor James Gregory, famous for his 'mixture', made up of magnesia powder, pulverised rhubarb and ginger. On the wall opposite the entrance to Woodburn House are two rectangular stones with the numbers 5 and 7 on them. These referred to the diameter of the water pipes bringing water from Comiston and Swanston respectively.

The fine wrought iron gates in view as the road bends round lead to the Astley Ainslie Hospital, opened in 1923 as a convalescent home for the Royal Infirmary. Just before the end of Canaan Lane, gates on the left lead to another secluded house, Woodville House, where James Wilson once lived. This man was remarkable for the fact that he wrote the entire section on Natural History in the 7th edition of the *Encyclopaedia Britannica*.

As you turn left into Newbattle Terrace the serenity of the scene is marred by the paraphernalia connected with the Woodcroft Telephone Exchange, once the site of a fine Baronial mansion. Turn right into Pitsligo Road and then right again into the high-walled Clinton Road. About half-way along on the left, a small dovecot can be seen behind a wall and behind that is visible East Morningside House with its white-washed walls and slate roofs. It was in this house that the novelist Susan Ferrier lived. Dubbed, 'Scotland's Jane Austen', she achieved fame with her novel, *Marriage,* published in 1818.

Further down on the right the pink turrets of a house called, 'Avalon' can be seen. Cross the road and look at the emblems in the gates to the Lodge. They show a curious combination of the scales of justice and an open book and above these a fist grasping holly. These are the coat of arms granted to the Green family and are to be seen in many of the books published by W. Green and Son, the legal publishers of Edinburgh.

Turn left into Whitehouse Loan whose right-hand side is dominated by the long building of St Margaret's Convent which was established in 1835 as the first Roman Catholic Convent in Scotland, after the Reformation. Further on down, also on the right, is James Gillespie's Girls School which incorporates within its walls, Bruntsfield House, one of the oldest mansions in the city. Unfortunately only glimpses of the building can be obtained through the gaps in the high wall.

Whitehouse Loan takes you back to the Meadows again and the end of the walk.

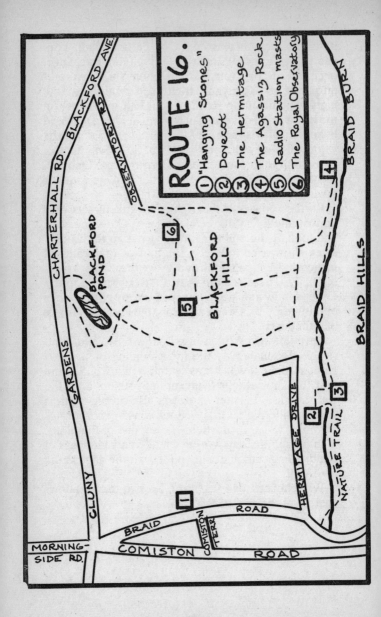

ROUTE 16.

① "Hanging Stones"
② Dovecot
③ The Hermitage
④ The Agassiz Rock
⑤ Radio Station masts
⑥ The Royal Observatory

BRAID BURN

BLACKFORD AVE.

OBSERVATORY RD.

CHARTERHALL RD.

BLACKFORD POND

⑥

BLACKFORD HILL

⑤

④

BRAID HILLS

GARDENS

③

②

NATURE TRAIL

HERMITAGE DRIVE

CLUNY

①

BRAID   ROAD

COMISTON TERR.

MORNING-SIDE RD.

COMISTON   ROAD

148

Route 16

THE HERMITAGE AND BLACKFORD HILL

This is a beautiful walk close to, and yet far removed in spirit, from the hurly burly of the city.

The walk begins at Comiston Terrace to the side of Comiston Road. This street quickly brings you to Braid Road where you should turn left and then stop almost immediately, for in front of No. 66 on the road, there are two large stones surrounded by bricks. These are called 'hanging stones' and in one of his essays, Robert Louis Stevenson recalls the old wive's tale that the stones were always damp with the blood of 2 men unjustly hanged on this spot, for stealing a mere 4d. But if you touch the stones you will find them quite dry and indeed there is little truth in the story. The two men, Thomas Kelly and Henry O'Neil, got away with considerable loot when they set upon and robbed a carter, David Loch, as he returned home to Biggar.

Retrace your steps past Comiston Terrace again and walk up Braid Road with the sight of the Braid Hills already in view. Just past Hermitage Drive turn left into a muddy drive past a gatehouse. This gatehouse is not what it seems, but is actually an old toll house which once stood at the foot of Morningside Road. In 1852 there was a public outcry against this toll which meant the citizens of Morningside had to pay 2d every time they wanted to go into the city centre. Their wrath bore fruit and a new toll house was built on the south bank of Jordan Burn, which was outside the city boundary. The old one was taken down and re-erected in exactly the same fashion on the spot you are now facing. If you look carefully you may be able to see the number 269 on the lintel at the back of the house. This refers to the house's previous incarnation when it was at 269 Morningside Road.

Cross over the fast flowing burn, the Braid Burn, and walk along the path which soon turns into a sweeping avenue lined by rhododendrons and all kinds of deciduous trees. As the gatehouse and cultivated greenery would suggest, we are now in the grounds of a house and are walking up the entrance drive of the building known as the Hermitage, hence the name of the road you passed earlier, Hermitage Drive. To the left, the lie of the land changes dramatically as the bank rises to form steep crags.

Just past the Public Conveniences the burn goes underground, so it is possible to double back on yourself and walk up the muddy track to steps which take you up to a curious two storey building high on the hill. From its external appearance its function may not be clear but this is in fact a dovecot from the 18th century. It is now shut up but inside there are two tapering chambers, shelved from top to toe to achieve a honeycomb effect and accommodate 1,965 pigeon holes, each of which is 10 inches square. On these crags there also used to be a castle but nothing is left of it now.

From the dovecot turn to your right and walk along until more steps take you down, just in front of the house known as the Hermitage. As Mrs Sellar, one of the frequent visitors to the Hermitage in the 19th century, said, 'it is indeed a lovely romantic spot . . . so far removed from every appearance of neighbourhood that it might have been a lodge in a vast wilderness'. Cleverly built into the lie of the land, this house was built for Charles Gordon of Cluny, in 1785 and designed by William Burn in the type of style used by the Adam Brothers.

It is thought that the fact there used to be a castle in

the vicinity may have influenced the style of architecture which at times resembles a miniature fortress, with pointed turrets on the corner of the walls and a battlemented top. In fact the 'wilderness' observed by Mrs Sellar is here somewhat tamed: when the house was built the lawn was levelled, the avenue we have just walked up was laid out, and an old corn mill on the banks of the burn was demolished. Before this house was built there was another house on the site which was owned by the Browns of Braid. This was also called, 'the Hermitage' and yet there seems to be no reliable explanation of the derivation of the name, and no traces of a hermitage have ever been found.

At first this spot seemed to bring bad luck to the inhabitants. One of the most famous owners of the first Hermitage was Sir William Dick who was an exceedingly prosperous merchant in Edinburgh but less successful in his political convictions. Because of his support for Covenanting principles, he was fined so heavily by Charles II that he ended his days in abject poverty, dying in the Fleet prison for debtors in London in 1655. The daughter, Joanna, of Charles Gordon, the first owner of the present house, married the 7th Earl of Stair. The marriage was a disaster and the Earl soon married again although not legally divorced. The poor Joanna pined away as a recluse in the Hermitage and bordered on insanity until her death in 1847.

Happier days were seen at the Hermitage when John Skelton and his wife took over the tenancy in 1868. Skelton was a famous historian and a writer under the pen name, 'Shirley', and in his time many famous visitors came to the Hermitage such as James Anthony Froude and Thomas Huxley, grandfather of the author Aldous Huxley. Later C. G. Barkla, Professor of Natural Philosophy at Edinburgh University lived there until 1937 when the house and its grounds were donated to the city. After years of neglect it is now being used as a countryside information centre.

Just beyond the house the burn emerges again making the scene even more picturesque. Following the river we go into a narrow valley between high crags and tall trees where at points as you walk along, it is difficult to know where rocks end and vegetation begins. Allowing for proprietorial exaggeration, we can see why Skelton writing as 'Shirley' said about this dell, 'our wood indeed is hardly so thick and tangled as that which enclosed the Sleeping Beauty'. The path criss-crosses the river and gradually the slopes get grassier while there are now less trees on the left. This is because they are on the rock of Blackford Hill whose thin soil is not hospitable to deciduous trees. Note the contrast with the different type of soil of the Braid Hills to the right.

As we reach the third bridge we begin to come out of the wood and we eventually leave the grounds of the Hermitage by a gate under a wooden rustic bridge. From here you can take the steps to the left up to Blackford Hill or, those with a geological interest, may wish to continue on to see the Agassiz rock. If so, follow the Braid Burn quietly running to the right. Pass through another gate and follow the path as it begins to rise. The Agassiz rock which stands to the left is a flat rock overhanging a small cave.

The rock got its name in 1840 when the then editor of *The Scotsman,* Charles Maclaren, showed the rock to Agassiz, a famous Swiss geologist who at once proclaimed, 'that is the work of the ice'. This proclamation is recorded on a plaque on the rock. The cave has been created from the cliff of andesite lava being worn away and if you look very carefully you can see that both the cliff and cave are grooved and ridged. These converging and diverging markings were formed when a great ice sheet, believed to have been as much as 1,000 feet thick, moved across Scotland from west to east and exerted a tremendous pressure on the rock underneath, causing it to have its present formation.

Unfortunately the old Blackford quarry prevents you from cutting across from here to Blackford Hill. In the 19th century the quarry was worked for old red sandstone which was used for road metal, particularly after 1831 when quarrying was stopped on Salisbury Crags under Arthur's Seat because it was ruining the natural lines of the hill. Of course the quarrying was not improving Blackford Hill either, and in 1852 protestors were finally successful in stopping it, particularly as the quarrying was disturbing the finely balanced instruments of the Royal Observatory on top of the hill.

Retrace your path back to the bridge, climb the steps to the right and follow the path which skirts around the hill. Just as houses come into view to the left, turn up right towards the masts on top of the hill. A steep climb takes you up to the summit where your efforts are rewarded by a fabulous view. Those who wish to take life easier can keep on the path a little longer and then fork right on a path which takes you round the shoulder of the hill. If you take the route to the top, at the summit you will have a panoramic view of the Braid Hills and then beyond them the Pentland Hills. Turn to your right and make your way towards the green towers of the Royal Observatory.

You can now go into the Observatory to find not only fine views but a display of telescopes, photographs of galaxies, stars, etc. The Observatory was opened on 7th April, 1896 when it was becoming obvious that the Observatory on Calton Hill was inadequate for the work in hand. The new Observatory benefited from a generous bequest of the instruments and astronomical library of the Earl of Crawford and Balcarres.

From the Observatory turn to the left and walk across the top of the hill until you come to the trig. point. From here you have another very fine view, this time of Arthur's Seat and the Castle, with the sea and Fife behind while there are open views to your back. It was from Blackford Hill that Sir Walter Scott describes Marmion looking at the mustering of the Scottish Army on Burgh Muir, just before marching off to their doom at the Battle of Flodden. Scott sets the scene:

Where the huge Castle holds its state,
And all the steep slope down,
Whose ridgy back heaves to the sky,
Piled deep and massy, close and high,
Mine own romantic town.

The houses which now cover the old Burgh Muir may detract somewhat from the scene but much is still just as Scott describes it.

Climb down the hill, another steep slope and rather gorse ridden, and you soon see Blackford Pond nestling under the hill. (The slope is less severe if you bear more to the right.) Steps take you down to the pond. Blackford Pond has been the host of Waverley Curling Club since its establishment in 1848 but, whether ice covered or not, the pond provides a very pleasant walk around it with a chance to see a profusion of fowl, duck, geese, moorhens etc. Halfway round the pond, a path takes you onto Charterhall Road where if you turn left and follow the road, now called Cluny Gardens, this brings you back to Morningside Road and the end of the walk.

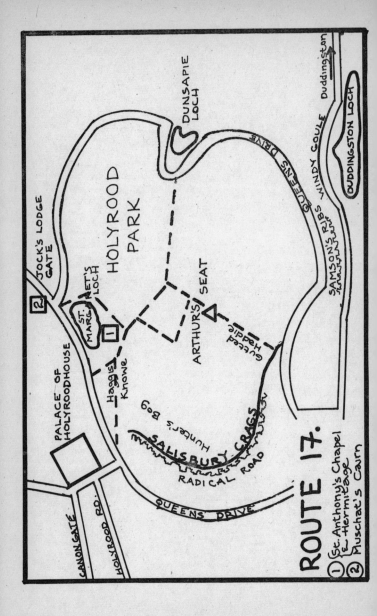

ROUTE 17.

① St. Anthony's Chapel & Hermitage
② Muschat's Cairn

DUNSAPIE LOCH

Duddingston

QUEENS DRIVE

SAMSON'S RIBS WINDY GOWLE

DUDDINGSTON LOCH

JOCK'S LODGE GATE

HOLYROOD PARK

ST. MARGARET'S LOCH

ARTHUR'S SEAT

Gutted Haddie

② [2]

① [1]

Haggis Knowe

Hunter's Bog

SALISBURY CRAGS

RADICAL ROAD

PALACE OF HOLYROODHOUSE

CANONGATE

HOLYROOD RD.

QUEENS DRIVE

156

Route 17

ARTHUR'S SEAT

Arthur's Seat is one of the greatest treasures of Edinburgh – its characteristic shape, like a brooding lion, dominates many parts of the city and its summit provides marvellous views over the surrounding countryside. Its ascent can be easily accomplished from Dunsapie Loch but if you choose there is also some fine walking and views to be obtained before the loch is reached.

Enter Holyrood Park at Holyrood Palace and almost in front of you take the steps up the hill which lead you onto the Radical Road. This path gets its name from the idea, promoted by Walter Scott, of setting discontented and destitute handloom weavers who had been thrown out of employment, to build the road. Thus occupied, it was argued, they would forget any radical feelings of protest which they might otherwise be harbouring. Nowadays this route can hardly be called a road for it is very narrow. But it soon begins to give you splendid views as the sea opens out behind Holyrood Palace and to the side, Edinburgh Castle stands sentinel over the city. Eventually you reach a plateau and, were it not for the buildings on your right, you could imagine yourself to be deep in the country.

To your left can be seen the damage left from the quarrying of the rock. By the end of the 18th century, quarrying had become big business with rock going to build the developments of the New Town and even being used in London. The Park's Hereditary Keeper, the Earl of Haddington, was doing very nicely from the affair since, when in 1831 the House of Lords finally agreed to a petition to stop the quarrying which was spoiling the line of the crags, the Keeper was compensated for the surrender of his office to the tune of £30,674, 1s 8d!

Salisbury Crags on which you are now standing are made up of great masses of greenstone set up in a volcanic explosion. They are said to take their name from the Earl of Salisbury who made ferocious raids against Scotland in the reign of Edward III. Some commentators have felt that naming the crags in this way sets them up as symbols of English aggression and Scottish humiliation.

As the road slopes down you can see the lion-like shape of Arthur's Seat. Geologically it is known that the rock is the core of an extinct volcano but the derivation of its name is in some doubt. Some have seen it as coming from the Celtic – Ard-na-Saigheid, meaning a height or flight of arrows possibly in reference to the archery which used to be practised on its slopes. Others have connected the hill with the famous King Arthur of Camelot and the Round Table.

At the bottom of the hill you meet another path onto which you should turn left. From here, you can either continue round the base of the hill, or turn sharp left and walk up 'Gutted Haddie', straight up towards the summit of Arthur's Seat. 'Gutted Haddie' was formed in 1744 when torrential rain tore a passage through the rock and eventually left a huge quantity of stones and gravel. As a result a wide cleft was formed in the rock looking like a cleaned out haddock spread out, hence its name. 'Gutted Haddie' provides the most exciting and arduous ascent to Arthur's Seat. Walking up its steep slopes leads to a healthy respect for Arthur's Seat which the author Robert Louis Stevenson called, 'a hill of magnitude, a mountain in virtue of its boldest design'. But be warned, about three quarters of the way up any semblance of a path disappears, and to get to the top you have to scramble over rocks which can be a little perilous if you are not careful. So if this does not appeal continue along to the gentle ascent from Dunsapie Loch where Lord Palmerston, at nearly 80, used to climb from.

To get to this walk join Queen's Drive, the boundary road around the park, which was built in 1844 as part of a scheme for improving the Park. The Queen in question was Queen Victoria who had a great love of Edinburgh and Scotland. From the drive you have a fine view of Duddingston and its loch over to the right. The road gently climbs to Dunsapie Loch which was created in its present form at the same time as the construction of the Queen's Drive. This spot, which is overlooked or guarded by Dunsapie Hill, provides a fine defensive site and there was a fort, some evidence of which still remains, here from pre-Roman times. From the loch a gentle grassy path takes you up towards Arthur's Seat although its last stages, when it joins the path from the right, can be a little slippery. This is also true of the rocky summit of Arthur's Seat.

The top of Arthur's Seat, at the 'head' of the 'lion' is one of two vents of the old volcano, the other is on the lower slopes or 'haunch' of the 'lion'. As you can see the summit where we are now standing actually has two peaks, one of which contains a direction indicator showing the major landmarks in your view. From this vantage point, 822 feet above sea level, on a clear day you can see as many as 15 peaks. Before Local Government Reorganisation in 1975 you would also have been able to see 12 counties but these have now been transformed into an amorphous mass of districts and regions. At your feet is the whole of Edinburgh, Old and New Town, and the port of Leith.

While you stand on this windswept spot you might like to spare a thought for an 18th century doctor James Graham, who believed that illness was a result of heat. Consequently he wore no woollen clothes and slept on a bare mattress even in winter. In order finally to prove his theory he wanted to build a house on the summit of Arthur's Seat which he considered to be suitably cold for his purposes. Mercifully for the future inhabitants of this house and for the beauty of this spot, his request was turned down.

It is easier to sympathise with Robert Burns who is depicted by his biographer as being inclined in springtime to lie prone on Arthur's Seat surveying the rising of the sun out of the sea in silent admiration. On a more scientific note, if you have a compass you can test the magnetic powers of the summit which are said to be so strong that the compass needle can be completely reversed.

Leave Arthur's Seat and retrace your steps towards Dunsapie Loch but before very long branch off to the left down the steep part of the hill. Gradually, well camouflaged by the rocks, the remains of St Anthony's Chapel come into view. Take the path to the left of the chapel past the long flat boulder, called St Anthony's Well. Although it bears little resemblance to a well now, water coming up from a spring below was once piped from here.

No-one seems to know exactly when St Anthony's Chapel was founded although it is thought most likely to date from the 15th century. The stone walls which you can see are all that remains of the chapel and hermitage which were probably set up by the Knights Hospitallers of St Anthony at Leith. The chapel, in a prominent place, could be seen by the sailors as they entered and left Leith and who could therefore offer up a prayer to St Anthony for their safe return. A path to the right of the chapel winds down to the lapping waters of St Margaret's Loch, again artificially created in the 19th century.

Once you reach the road again you can either turn left towards Holyrood Palace and leave the Park by the way you came in, or you can turn to the right and then take the left-hand fork to the East or Jock's Lodge Gate. Just by the exit to the park is a heap of stones to the left called Muschat's Cairn which has many stories to tell. This cairn used to be situated on Hunter's Bog under Arthur's Seat but it was moved in 1822 to its present site in order that George IV might see it without wetting his feet. In its original position the cairn marked the site of the cruel murder by Nicol Muschat of his wife in 1720. Muschat tried several times to murder the poor woman including poisoning her but to no avail, so eventually he stabbed her to death on Arthur's Seat. It is said that so vicious and frequent were his stabbings that his wife called out 'O Man, it is done now; you need not give me more!' Sir Walter Scott related the story in his *The Heart of Midlothian* where he also used the Cairn for an assignation between Jeanie Deans and her lover.

You can either leave the park by the gate or retrace your steps back to the Holyrood Palace exit. If you do the latter you pass the old St Margaret's Well on the right which was transferred here from Restalrig in 1862.

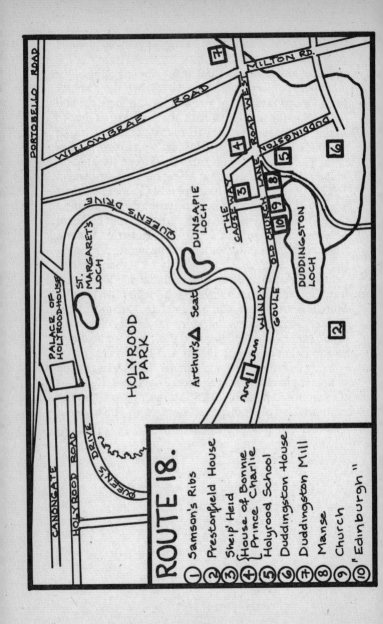

ROUTE 18.

① Samson's Ribs
② Prestonfield House
③ Sheip' Heid
④ House of Bonnie Prince Charlie
⑤ Holyrood School
⑥ Duddingston House
⑦ Duddingston Mill
⑧ Manse
⑨ Church
⑩ "Edinburgh"

Route 18

DUDDINGSTON VILLAGE

Duddingston is one of the lovliest and most surprising parts of Edinburgh – a picturesque loch-side village little touched by the ravages of time and yet within easy walking distance of the city centre.

To walk to the village enter Holyrood Park by Holyrood Park Road, near the University Pollock Halls of Residence. Immediately you enter branch off to the right along the lower road in the park. As you walk you soon come to a curious formation in the rock which, with its long thin lines like the bones of a giant, has been aptly named, Samson's Ribs. These are actually great columns of basalt cut by nature into regular forms and towering some 80 or 90 feet above the road.

Looking down to the right you can see Prestonfield House, built in 1687 as the home of the Dick family, and now a hotel. As you pass through the stretch known as Windy Goule – if there is any wind about you will soon realise that this is also appropriately called – you soon come into view of Duddingston Loch.

The loch is fed by water from a spring below Samson's Ribs, colourfully named, the Wells o' Wearie, and used to be much larger, about twice its present size. Indeed it is thought possible that a bronze age village, then named, Traverlen, was once built on piles in the loch. But over the years the water has silted up and filled with reeds so that today the loch is only 30 acres in area and even at its deepest point, only 10 feet deep. The reeds on the loch's southern edge make it a marvellous breeding ground for birds and since 1925 the loch has been conserved as a bird sanctuary.

Keen ornithologists will be interested to know of the birds such as the pochard which first bred here in 1926 and the great crested grebe in 1937. Other rare birds also visit the loch such as the red throated diver and the smew whilst more common birds such as, mallards, crested ducks and snipe are frequent visitors. The swans on the loch are reputedly descendants of those put there in the 17th century.

As we walk on the picturesque sight of the church standing above the loch comes into view and we can begin to see why Duddingston was once described as, 'a mere toy village, breathing soft smoke pillars, breathing fruit tree fragrance . . . silent as Pompei itself'. But unlike Vesuvius, the once volcanic Arthur's Seat, is now extinct and harmless! Looking back to Arthur's Seat we can see the lines of old cultivated terraces from prehistoric times.

Leave the park through a gate to the left of the road at the exit. As a complete contrast from the wide open space of the park we are now in a narrow lane surrounded by high walls. This is the Causeway which soon comes out into the open again at an attractive whitewashed pub, the Sheip' Heid. Although this building dates from the 19th century there is reputed to have been a pub here from the 14th century.

According to tradition the pub gets its name from the day in 1500 when James VI, a frequent visitor from nearby Holyrood, presented the landlord with a ram's head decorated in gold. The choice of a ram's head was appropriate for singed sheep's head, either baked or boiled, was a popular local dish and must often have provided a meal for the King. When a sheep was caught on Arthur's Seat the body was sent to Edinburgh, leaving the head in Duddingston to be eaten. Inside the pub at the back is the oldest skittle alley in Scotland. The records of the skittle club date back as far as the eighteenth century and its regalia include a curious motley collection of objects such as a silver snuff box, a large ram's head and a Bristol blue decanter.

Continue along the Causeway keeping the Sheip' Heid to your right. In the 18th century there were weavers' cottages to your right and left, housing the workers of a thriving industry. In 1763 more than 30 looms were producing a type of flaxen cloth called, Duddingston Hardings. However, the industry could not keep up with rival competition and declined quickly so that by 1845 there were no weavers left.

At the entrance to the lane on your left, notice the stone cart tracks, a reminder of the days before the advent of the motor car. Behind the wall on the right, used to be the village green but it is built up now. Further down on the left is Hawthorn Brae, now owned by the Church of Scotland. This handsome house with Greek Doric pillars enjoys, like much of Duddingston, a superb backdrop of Arthur's Seat and Holyrood Park. The white-washed, single-storeyed houses on the corner are modern reproductions of the old weavers' cottages.

Just round the corner on the left is the red-roofed house where Bonnie Prince Charlie held a council of war on 21st September 1745. His troops were garrisoned there before their victory at the Battle of Prestonpans. The house has recently been restored and is to become a museum of Jacobite relics.

Turn left into Duddingston Road West, cross over and take the path leading up to the left of Holyrood School with the golf course on your left. As you walk up the path look to your left to see a small temple-like building with pillars surmounted by a dome. This is one of the last remnants of a landscaped garden and gives a clue that these were once the grounds of a house – Duddingston House. In 1750 this land was laid out by James Robertson in the style of the famous landscape gardener, Capability Brown, into a 200 acre park with lakes, temples and grottos. In 1873 the land was sold to the Benhar Coal Company and became overgrown but was restored somewhat when it became Duddingston Golf Course.

If you take the path to the right leading to Mansion House Hotel, you will soon come to the original Duddingston House, now a hotel. This fine blue building was built for the Earl of Abercorn to the design of William Chambers between 1763–68. It has an elegant Corinthian portico with fluted pillars and an impressive interior staircase. In a curious piece of design only the main rooms were in the house, the rest being in a detached wing linked to the stables. The house's first owner was said to have been rather a stiff-necked, dry individual who, when complimented on how well his trees were growing, gave the acid reply, 'they have nothing else to do'.

Retrace your steps back to the main drive and cross the Braid Burn. Stop for a moment to appreciate the superb countryside and as you look back to Arthur's Seat it is easy to see why the 14th century parson, William Bennet, remarked of Duddingston, 'the most beautiful and picturesque scenery expands before it and on every side . . .' The drive joins the road at elegant gates set in blue bowed walls which are decorated by 2 circular plaques.

Turn left and walk down Milton Road until you cross the burn again, now called the Figgate Burn. If you cross the road you will see it tumbling down on its way to Figgate Pond. At the crossroads continue on down Willowbrae Road past the forge with its curious stepped roof.

Take a path to the right which takes you down to what were once flourishing flour and barley mills. These were established in 1790 at a cost of £6,000 and produced flour which was sold as far as the Orkneys and Shetlands. The mills were situated by the burn which was then divided into several lades or channels to provide the power for the water wheels. The wheels stopped working in 1950 and unfortunately were badly damaged by fire in 1954. Now the mill buildings are used as commercial premises.

Retrace your steps to the road, turn left and then right at the cross roads into Duddingston Road West which takes you back to the old village. There are some lovely old houses on this road, in differing styles. One for instance, looks rather like a fortress with the left hand side of the house ending in a castle turret. Lochside House is another very attractive house but the most interesting house is the Manse on the left. Under an ashtree in the garden, now only a bit of bark, Sir Walter Scott is thought to have written much of his famous novel, *The Heart of Midlothian*.

The tenant of the Manse at the time was Reverend John Thomson who, apart from his clerical duties as Minister of Duddingston, was a fine artist and is often seen as the father of Scottish scene painting. Thomson was visited by many famous contemporaries of whom the most celebrated, the artist Turner, is reputed to have confided to Thomson, 'by God, though, I envy you that piece of water'. The Manse does indeed have a marvellous position overlooking the loch although, as it is in private hands, we cannot see the exact view which produced such feelings of envious longing.

Duddingston Church, the oldest building in the village, dates from the 12th century and is superbly situated on a mound above the loch. Before you go into the churchyard look to the right of the gate where there are four stone steps by the wall. This was probably a 'loupin on stane' which was invaluable for rather fat or elderly parishioners when they wanted to mount their horses after church. Behind this is a more fearsome object, a 'joug's collar', made of iron which was used as a form of punishment in the sober 17th century. When anyone was caught drunk, blaspheming or merely not going to church they were put in sackcloth and attached by the collar to the church wall, as a warning to all potential sinners.

Entering the churchyard you will find an octagonal tower which was used in the 19th century to guard graves from 'body snatchers' who used to steal newly buried bodies and sell them for medical purposes. Metal grilles and large stones were also put over graves as further deterrents. But one would-be body snatcher was put off the trade in a more effective manner. When he unearthed the body of a young lady recently buried in the churchyard he found the 'corpse' sneezed and subsequently lived to tell the tale!

The church itself was originally of Norman design with a plain nave but a north aisle was added in 1631 when the windows were enlarged into a perpendicular style. In the north wall of the chancel is a small recess which it is thought may have been used as a 'leper's squint'. Lepers outside were able to see the minister as he preached but were separated from the congregation, who were thus free from contamination.

Walking down towards the park you can see a small building by the lochside. This was built in 1825 and the first floor was rented by Rev. Thomson as a studio. The minister cleverly called the building, 'Edinburgh', so that when casual visitors called to see him in the Manse the servants were able to say he had gone to Edinbugh, thereby confounding the caller and at the same time saving their souls from the dangers of falsehood.

Duddingston Loch was a great centre of curling and the headquarters of the curling society were located in the ground floor of 'Edinburgh'. In 1838 a 'Grand Club' was formed with strict rules governing everything from the playing of the game to the behaviour of the players. For instance anyone uttering an oath was fined 3d and the fine was doubled if politics were brought up. In the 19th century the sport declined in popularity and some of the old curling ground is now used as a bird sanctuary.

Leave Duddingston and enter the park again. You can either go back the way you came or take the steps leading up the hill to the right. At the top of the steps take the track to the left which takes you to Queen's Drive (named after Queen Victoria). From the loch you can climb over Arthur's Seat (see page 157), or return on the upper road to the left to the gate by Holyrood Park Road.

Or you can turn to the right and do a circular tour of Holyrood Park. If you follow this route you will have fine views over to the sea, first of Portobello and then sweeping round to Leith. The road bends round to the beautiful St Margaret's Loch which presents a lovely scene of seagulls and ducks flying above waters, constantly whipped up by the wind. If you choose you can leave the Park by the Holyrood Palace exit or continue round to the gate you first entered the Park by.

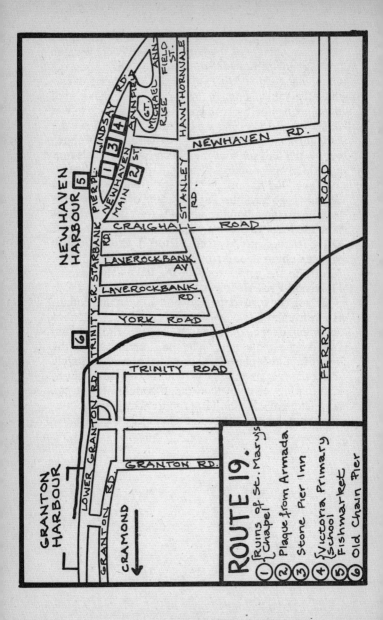

NEWHAVEN HARBOUR

GRANTON HARBOUR

GRANTON RD.
GRANTON RD.
LOWER GRANTON RD.

CRAMOND

TRINITY CR.
STARBANK RD.

LINDSAY RD.
PIER PL.
5
MAIN ST.
NEWHAVEN
1
2 ST.
3
4
ANN PIER
GT. MICHAEL RISE
ANN ST.
FIELD ST.
HAWTHORNVALE

NEWHAVEN RD.

STANLEY RD.

CRAIGHALL ROAD

LAVEROCKBANK AV.

LAVEROCKBANK RD.

YORK ROAD
6

TRINITY ROAD

ROAD

FERRY ROAD

ROUTE 19.

① Ruins of St. Marys Chapel
② Plaque from Armada
③ Stone Pier Inn
④ Victoria Primary School
⑤ Fishmarket
⑥ Old Chain Pier

Route 19

NEWHAVEN AND THE SHORE TO GRANTON

Newhaven was once famed for its fishwives and their cries of 'wha'll buy my caller herrin?' Alas these are no more but Newhaven still retains its own distinct character.

Begin your walk facing the sea at the bottom of Craighall Road, and turn right into Newhaven Main Street. You don't have to go very far before you realise that the atmosphere and style of architecture here is very different from anywhere else in Edinburgh.

Newhaven provided a refuge for Protestants exiled by, or fleeing from, Catholic persecution in the Lowlands, particularly in the reign of Philip II of Spain. So it was that many of the original inhabitants of the settlement were Flemish and Belgian and this is reflected in the type of houses that they built. It also used to show in their dialect, in their chief occupation which was fishing as it had been in their native land, and in the typical dress of the fishwives with their many petticoats striped in contrasting colours. With the decline of the local fishing industry this sight, unfortunately, is no longer to be seen.

Newhaven is so called to distinguish it from the Old Haven or Blackness, the sea port of Linlithgow. Its history has seen a series of enterprises flourishing for a while and then stopping. In 1551 James IV aimed to make it a great shipbuilding centre but the plan died with him at his death at the Battle of Flodden in 1513. In the 18th and 19th centuries it rose to some prominence as a ferry port but was then eclipsed by Leith and Granton on either side. But all the while fishing, particularly for herring and oysters, went on.

It is best to walk down the street on the right and so you can look across to the houses on the left, most of which have been recently and successfully reconstructed; the old houses on the right having been cleared away. Notice the unusual gabled house, colour-washed yellow at the bottom and rough stone at the top. Along from this are the typical houses of 18th century Newhaven which housed the fishermen. Notice their common features of red pantiled (curved tiles) roofs, and whitewashed walls with brown window surrounds.

Cross the road and walk down the court on your left, Westmost Court, and notice the old wall on the right. This is the remains of a chapel built by James IV in the 16th century and dedicated to St Mary. Because of this Newhaven was known for a time as 'Our Lady's Port of Grace' or Maryport. The chapel was mostly destroyed in the Earl of Hertford's invasion of Leith in 1544. While you are in the close, notice the houses with outside wooden stairs, another distinguishing feature of Newhaven architecture.

Return to Main Street and just after Lamb's Court cross the road to a small courtyard. There on the wall of a house is a curious looking plaque showing the date 1588 at the top, underneath is a ship flying the St Andrew's flag, and below this is an inscription, 'In the Neam of God'. At the bottom there is a Latin inscription which has been roughly translated as 'Valour guided by the stars, can traverse both land and sea'. This plaque marks the local tradition that the Newhaven fishermen played a part in the defeat of the Spanish Armada against the English in 1588. Because of the persecution suffered by the men they would have had good reason to hate Philip and the Spanish, and some coins from the ships of the

Spaniards have been found along this coast, but otherwise there is little historical proof of this tale.

To the left of Main Street is Fisherman's Square, another reminder of the means of the livelihood of the village. For centuries Newhaven was famous for its oysters, even coming to blows, successfully, with nearby Prestonpans in 'the battle of the boats' about their rights to the oyster beds. It is recorded that the battle was ended after 'much hurt being received on both sides'. By 1836 over 50 Newhaven boats, each with a crew of five, were working dredging up the oysters, but the industry rapidly declined in the 19th century, probably because of over-fishing. In 1886 six million oysters were landed at Newhaven, by 1890 this number had shrunk to 2,000 and by 1900 the trade was dead. In 1793 herring began to be netted and the basis was laid for a highly profitable fishing industry which has only declined in this century.

Appropriately enough, on the left of the square, is a fishmongers. At the bottom is a pub named, the Stone Pier Inn, recalling the days when Newhaven was a busy ferry port in the late 18th, early 19th centuries. Newhaven formed part of the route from Edinburgh to Aberdeen while the London and Edinburgh Steam Packet Company had sailings every Wednesday and Saturday from Newhaven to London. It was at Newhaven that Sir Walter Scott arrived on his last trip from London. But the pier had certain disadvantages including the fact that it was sometimes difficult or even impossible to approach it at low tide. In 1838 the deep harbour of Granton was opened and Newhaven once again became just a fishing village.

Returning to Main Street, notice the way in which the houses, of the same style as before, now have their outside staircases fronting onto the street. The line of cottages is broken by the unusual building of the Auld Haven whose layout of wooden beams creates a curious effect on its facade. At the back of Peacock Court to the left is Ye Olde Peacock Hotel. This has a long and interesting history which began in 1767 when Thomas Peacock, a Vintner by trade, petitioned Edinburgh for the use of some cottages, in which he produced mouth-watering fish meals. In the next century the trade was carried on by Mrs Clark who added the present building and served 'Real and Original Clark's Newhaven Fish Dinners'.

Back on Main Street opposite the Victorian School was once the Free Fishermen Park, now covered up by a tenement building. An important feature of Newhaven life was the Free Fishermen's Society which existed from 1572. Basically a relief organisation for the poor among them, the Society also protected fishing rights and helped keep the village a close-knit, exclusive community. In 1817 the Society brought in rules to prevent people from becoming members unless they were 'the lawful sons of fishermen whose names were clear in the book'.

Further down on the right, Great Michael Rise, commemorates another memorable event in Newhaven's history. Although James IV's grandiose ambitions for Newhaven were not realised, he did manage to have a ship built there which has become legendary for its great size, being called 'ane varie monstrous great schip'. According to one historian it needed so much timber that building the ship, 'wasted all the woods of Fife'. In fact she was apparently so big that it was impossible to navigate her although she was good for defence. To test her out James had a canon ball fired at her and it is reported that her 10 feet thick oak timbers 'hardly shuddered'. Although Great Michael Rise is a new development, its architecture, with colour-washed houses and slate roofs, fits in well with the rest of Newhaven, and has been justly commended for good design by the Saltire Society. Next door in New Lane, the outside staircases match the earlier wooden ones on the houses in Main Street.

Turn left into Newhaven Place where there is an entry to the Leith Docks which is prohibited to the general public. Walk back along the sea-front parallel to Main Street, noticing more reconstructed houses until you come to the old Newhaven harbour. On the right, the long thin building is the old fishmarket built in 1896 to be the most important on the Forth, and it still operates daily. The harbour itself was reconstructed in 1876 and a sea wall with a light-house was added in 1881. It was here that the herring were landed which have been immortalised in Baronness Nairne's song, 'Wha'll buy my caller herrin?' ('caller' means fresh).

Wha'll buy my caller herrin?
They're bonnie fish and halesome faring,
Wha'll buy my caller herrin?
New drawn from the Forth.

The commonplace sight of fishwives carrying a heavy creel (basket) of fish from door to door in Edinburgh is no longer to be seen, nor is any fish landed at Newhaven. Now the harbour is a sleepy place used mainly for pleasure craft.

If you wish to explore the shore further there is a pleasant walk from here to Granton, the newer harbour. Continue along by the sea noticing more 18th century houses such as the one, topped by a clock, which overlooks the harbour. Further along, the roads going up the hill at right angles to the street, such as Laverockbank Road, contain some fine 19th century houses. One of these, No. 46, was lived in for a time by Sir James Young Simpson who discovered chloroform and demonstrated its benefits for operations.

Further down on the right is the Old Chain Pier pub which like the Stone Pier Inn marks the former days of Newhaven as a ferry port. A chain suspension pier, 500 feet long, was opened in 1821 in preparation for the visit of King George IV in 1822. For a while it was used by steam packets travelling up and down the coast but it too had to bow to the superior advantages of Granton, and finally in 1898 it was blown down.

Just before the road bends round to the left to go under a bridge, continue on the path by the shore. Away from the traffic this is a pleasant walk by the sea, until the track ends and you have to go through a tunnel back to the main road. Turn right and walk by the old railway line which was extended out here in 1848, and still carries occasional freight traffic. The line formed a vital link in the railway ferry to Burnt-island on the other side of the Forth. This was the first train ferry in the world (with carriages run onto rails on the ships), and closed on the opening of the Forth Bridge in 1890. As you walk on, the unmistakeable sight of the green tanks of Granton Gas Works, opened at the turn of the century, comes into view.

Just opposite Wardie's steps another tunnel takes you back onto the foreshore where there is a view of the harbour. Later on the harbour is mostly hidden from sight by all the docks and industrial buildings, and so this is a good point to see the harbour from. Granton harbour was begun in 1837 to meet the growing demand for a deep-water harbour which would allow large boats to sail right up to the pier. Much of the money and enthusiasm for the project came from the Duke of Buccleuch who owned the land.

In 1842 work started on the East and West break-waters which were to protect the pier and provide a safe harbour. Granton quickly became an important ferry port and it was here that Queen Victoria arrived and left on her visit to Edinburgh in 1842. With the opening of the Forth Bridge in 1890 this side of Granton's activities declined, but by then it was firmly established as an important commercial harbour, exporting coal and importing esparto grass for the manufacture of paper. By this time the trawling industry was also beginning to get going. Granton still remains the base of a trawler fleet as well as being an important industrial and commercial dock, while the Royal Forth Yacht Club is based on the eastern harbour, nearest you.

Go back to the road and keeping on Lower Granton Road you pass the Granton depot of the Northern Lighthouse Board which is marked out by the lighthouse lantern at the top. On the right the wall breaks down into a fence to allow you to see across to the harbour. Further down on the left notice the house on the corner with an elaborate stone balcony. Follow this round and it takes you into Granton Square, which was built in 1838 while the harbour was being constructed. It still retains an air of elegance particularly in the grand house which is now the HMS Claverhouse, housing the Royal Naval Reserve Forth Division.

From Granton Square it is possible to walk along the shore to another smaller harbour at Cramond. The last stretch of the walk is magnificent but the first part, along West Harbour Road and then West Shore Road is not recommended since for much of the way you are walking through an industrial estate. It is therefore advisable to catch a bus most of the way down West Shore Road and get off by the grassy area to the right, just as the road bends round to the left. From here you have a beautiful walk along a broad path formed in the 1930s when land was reclaimed from the sea and protected by a high wall, and the parkland which already existed was put at the public's disposal.

As you walk you look out to the bay to the towers of the fortress-like looking island of Inchmickery and the larger mass of Cramond Island. To the left the view is enlivened by the imposing facades of several old houses above on the bank, such as Craigroyston and Muirhouse. Further on, the path is dotted by curiously shaped pine trees until you come out in a green, and the cars parked above bring you back to civilisation. In the last stretch of the walk which is particularly beautiful you can see glimpses of Cramond House and Tower through the trees, while further down the coast, Barnbougle Castle stands out behind Dalmeny Woods. The esplanade brings you out by the beginning of the causeway to Cramond Island, at the foot of Cramond Village. If you still have the energy you might like to refresh yourself at the Cramond Inn to the left, and then walk over to Cramond Island (see page 181).

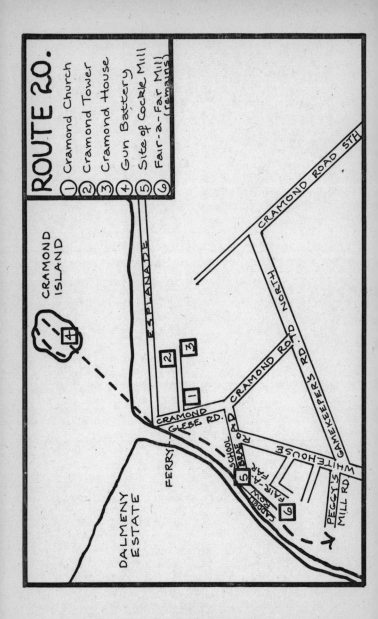

ROUTE 20.

① Cramond Church
② Cramond Tower
③ Cramond House
④ Gun Battery
⑤ Site of Cockle Mill
⑥ Fair-a-Far Mill
   (remains)

CRAMOND ISLAND

ESPLANADE

CRAMOND ROAD STH

CRAMOND RD. NORTH

CRAMOND ROAD

GAMEKEEPERS RD.

CRAMOND GLEBE RD.

FERRY

DALMENY ESTATE

SCHOOL RD

FAIR-A-FAR

CADDEL ROW

PEGGY'S MILL RD.

WHITEHOUSE

Route 20

CRAMOND ISLAND AND VILLAGE

Cramond is one of the most picturesque spots on the Forth. Now a tranquil village it was once the hub of a thriving industry.

A word of advice. If you wish to do the part of the walk which goes out to Cramond Island, check on the time of the tides first for it is approached by a causeway which is covered at high tide.

Start your walk at the top of Cramond Glebe Road, and walk down the street until you come to the church behind a wall on your right. Before going into the churchyard look across the road at a whitewashed house which, as its name proclaims, was the old schoolhouse of Cramond. This was opened in 1778 and replaced an even smaller school with only one room which was housed in a thatched building in the churchyard.

The history of Cramond Church or Kirk is bound up with the Roman occupation of the area, signs of which we shall see shortly. When the Christians of the 6th century wanted to build a place of worship they used the Principia or the main block of the Roman fort as the site. In 1656 a new church was built on the same site, using the old tower of the 15th century and 14th century stone. Since then it has been extended with south and north aisles being added.

The church itself is most attractive with its old tower and round the back, a stone slabbed roof. In the churchyard is buried Jock Howieson, who, according to the story, is said to have rescued James V from gypsies who attacked the King while hunting in the forest. The King who was disguised at the time, invited his rescuer to an event in Holyrood Palace but the invitation was couched in such a way as to give no hint of his real identity. Howieson was naturally amazed to arrive at the Palace and discover who this mysterious gentleman really was.

While you are in the churchyard notice the iron tomb 'stones' which reflect the significance of the iron trade to 18th and 19th century Cramond. Inside the church in the gallery, stands a chair which was used by Queen Victoria when she came to visit her mother, the Duchess of Kent, who was living at Cramond House nearby.

As you leave the churchyard and turn in the next entrance you will be able to see signs of the old Roman fort. Unlike most of Edinburgh, Cramond played some part in Roman Britain and her name reflects this. 'Cramond' is a contraction of 'Caer Almond' or 'Caer Amon' which means the fort on the river. In 142 A.D. the Romans built a fort and harbour here as part of their defensive line, the Antonine Wall, stretching from the Forth to the Clyde. Cramond's part was to act as a fortified harbour and store for supplies. Outside the fort a native village grew up inhabited by the Votadini or Goddodin who spoke an early form of Welsh.

After 15 years the Romans withdrew but returned again in the same century. The fort was restored at the beginning of the next century by Emperor Septimus Severus and remained under some form of Roman influence right up to the 6th century. The fort was discovered and excavated in 1954 and many items were found such as Roman coins, altars, pottery etc. These finds are on show in the Huntly House Museum in the Canongate in the Royal Mile. Now the excavations are mostly covered up but the lines of the fort have been traced on the ground and a map of the fort's layout confirms the church's position on the Roman Principia.

Walk down the path until you pass a curious tall stone tower on your left. This is the sole remnant of the old palace of the Bishops of Dunkeld. The exact age of the palace is uncertain, but it is thought it may date back as far as the 11th or 12th century and was certainly in existence by the 15th century. It was the Bishops of Dunkeld who gave Cramond the name of Cramond Episcopi (Bishop's Cramond), as opposed to Cramond Regis, further in shore, which was the property of the King. The tower is being restored and used by a taxidermist.

Continue on the path and you soon come to the imposing Cramond House. The rear part of the house was built in 1680 for John Inglis who was a merchant in Edinburgh. The classically styled front was added by another member of the family in 1771. Walking three-quarters the way round the house, notice the elaborate staircase which looks rather curious as it now leads up to a window.

Standing by the house and looking through the trees to the sea we can appreciate Queen Victoria's comment on her visit here, 'we paid dear Mamma a visit at her really charming residence at Cramond, quite near the sea, with beautiful trees and very cheerful'.

Retrace your steps back to the road and walk down the steep slope. Soon you come to picturesque white-washed cottages on the left with gaps in the row allowing glimpses of the river below. These houses, now looking almost too neat and clean to be real, once housed the workers of the mills situated all along the river. Built in the 18th century, the houses were restored in 1961 and all are in the same style with black surrounds to the windows and red tiled roofs. These cottages, together with those by the river below, are virtually all that is left of a once thriving village. In 1826 Lady Torphichen from Cramond

House decided to knock down half the village to the East of Cramond Glebe Road, and Cramond has never recovered from this piece of aristocratic vandalism.

On the right-hand side of the road you soon come to Cramond Inn, a very handsome building which is completely in keeping with the character of the cottages. The oldest part of the inn, facing onto the sea, was built in 1670, and the rest was added later in 1887.

The road bends round to the left down to the river front. To get to Cramond Island walk to the right until you come to the causeway by the side of the rather unsightly submarine barrier. At this point note the rather mystifying sign warning against eating mussels, the reasons for this become clearer later on. Walk down the causeway until you come to a board giving the times of high and low tide. It is vital that you take note of these to avoid being stranded, for most of the path from now is covered at high tide.

The path, now consisting of stones placed on a pipe, can feel a little hazardous as the water laps at your feet. As you look down you can see beds upon beds of mussels, hence the notice on the mainland. The water may be too polluted to allow you to eat the shellfish, but the pools of water with seagulls flying aloft, and behind you the lines of the shore, make a very tranquil picture. As you near the island the path once again becomes a proper road until you reach the shores of the island.

Cramond Island was given to the monks of St Colme in 1181 and in the 14th century the Pope had to intervene in a dispute over the ownership of the island. It is strange to think that this island, now deserted, together with Inchmickery, another small island further out to sea, once formed a separate parish of their own.

The island was once the scene of an experiment in stock-rearing conducted by the British Wool Society. An experimental type of Shetland sheep was placed on the island to test its survival chances, but the experiment proved to be a failure and the sheep were sent back to the mainland.

If you walk up onto the top of the island to the right, you will find evidences of another use which the island has been put to. Facing out to sea is an old gun battery and some of the old gun emplacements can still be seen. In the war Cramond Island, together with other forts along the coast, formed an inner line of defences against the submarines and acted as a site for guns and searchlights.

Coming away from the fort walk up onto the crest of the hill where a ruined house, now fighting a losing battle with the undergrowth, is a reminder of the days when Cramond Island was inhabited. From here walk over to the road which takes you to more mementos from the war. It is worth going in one or two since they contain some interesting relics such as the curious metal blocks jutting up from the floor. These huts were probably used for storage. Further round to the left we come to the other shore and more pre-fabs. Judging by their shape and position these were probably more gun positions or lookouts. Below these buildings is a form of harbour with some old mooring places. Looking out to sea you can detect the curious island of Inchmickery which has been very aptly described as 'a great Dreadnought at sea'.

From here you can walk round the shore and back to the causeway which takes you back to the mainland proper. From here bear round to the right to the mouth of the Almond River where you have a choice of two fine walks. You can either take the ferryboat across the river and walk through the beautiful woods of the Dalmeny Estate to Queensferry. Or you can follow the route outlined below which takes you along the riverbank.

As you walk by the river you are likely to be disturbed by nothing more noisy than the members of the Cramond Boat Club tinkering with their boats or families out for a stroll. But this would not have been the case a couple of hundred years earlier.

By the end of the 18th century, Cramond, blessed with a sea-port and a source of power from the river, had established itself as a thriving centre of iron manufacture, and the air would have been loud with the noise of the forge hammer pounding the metal and black from the dust of the mills. There were grain mills here as early as 1178 and from 1752 these mills were used to roll and cut imported bar-iron and re-forge scrap iron. Cramond was particularly famous for its nail and spade manufacture; 3,000 tons of nails were made here in 1770, but it also made barrel-hoops, pans for the salt works, handles etc. The mills were badly hit by the recession following the Napoleonic Wars with France, 1793–1815, and by the time they got going again they were too out-moded to do well, especially as steam was beginning to replace water as a form of power. But some mills did continue and diversified their activities, particularly into paper-making while as late as 1939 furniture was being made on the river. Now those mills which have not disappeared completely are in ruins.

Follow the path along the wooded banks of the river with views across to Lord Rosebery's Dalmeny estate. Just as houses come into view the site of the old mill-lade, built to power the mills, can be seen.

When we come to the houses and grassy bank we have reached the site of the old Cockle Mill and the limit to which the sea reaches at high tide. The main building to survive from the mill complex was the office block which has now been converted into an extremely attractive house. The mill itself stood on the grassy bank in front and was the main rolling and slitting mill used in the production of such goods as spades. Just beyond this, in the river, is the remains of a weir, now all broken down together with the small dock which was used by the ships supplying the mills.

As you walk on the left you pass some outhouses of the old mill and old cottages in Caddell's Row which once housed the mill-workers. The manager lived in a house high up on the bank, removed from the grime of the mills.

A little further down you come to the quite dramatic weir. These weirs were used to increase the head, and therefore force, of the river so it could turn the water wheels. Standing by the weir are the remains of the old Fair-A-Far Mill, now an empty shell with two long arched walls. Just below the mill, in the river you can see slag from the mill whilst across on the other side of the bank, at the level of the weir, you can see a horizontal row of holes. These are all that is left from a tramline jutting out over the river, which connected the mill to Craigie Quarry further upstream. A tramline also connected this mill with Cockle Mill downstream but no traces of this are visible.

Further up the path it is no longer possible to walk by the river and you have to climb steps onto a higher path although after a while steps take you back to the river's edge. Shortly after this there are two signposts pointing up and down stream. Here you can either continue upstream to the picturesque Cramond Brig and beyond or fork left up a muddy path between new houses. This becomes Peggy's Mill Road, named after yet another mill, and eventually brings you out into Whitehouse Road. From here you can turn left and walk back to Cramond Village or turn right and take a bus back to the city centre.

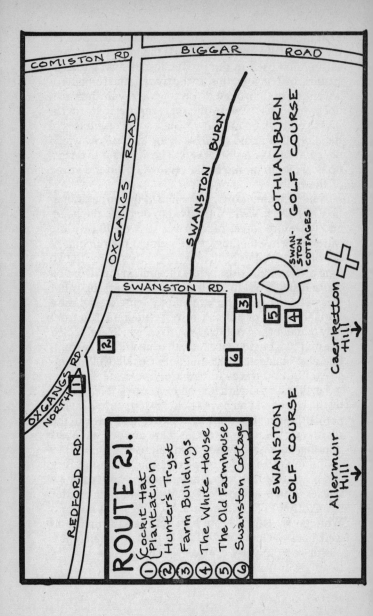

COMISTON RD. BIGGAR ROAD

OXGANGS ROAD

SWANSTON BURN

LOTHIANBURN GOLF COURSE

SWANSTON RD.

SWAN-
STON
COTTAGES

OXGANGS
NORTH RD.

REDFORD RD.

SWANSTON GOLF COURSE

Caerketton Hill →

Allermuir Hill →

ROUTE 21.

① Cockit Hat
    Plantation
② Hunter's Tryst
③ Farm Buildings
④ The White House
⑤ The Old Farmhouse
⑥ Swanston Cottage

Route 21

SWANSTON VILLAGE

Swanston still retains most of the charm and beautiful rural setting which made it so beloved of Robert Louis Stevenson, whose family had a summer home here, and whose presence still seems to linger on.

Approach the village from the junction of Oxgangs Road and Redford Road, by the curious clump of trees known as the Cockit Hat Plantation, on account of its shape. Turning right into Oxgangs Road you pass by the pub, the Hunter's Tryst. According to the fancy of Robert Louis Stevenson and others, this used to be haunted by Satan. It was also the meeting place of the Six Foot Club whose members were all over 6 feet tall.

Carry on and turn right into Swanston Road. Immediately you are confronted with the hills in front of you, as Stevenson said when describing the approach to Swanston, 'straight above the hills climb 1,000 feet into the air'. To the right of you as you walk are ploughed fields and to the other side, the new parts of Swanston which are fortunately separated from the old village.

At first the only noise which is likely to disturb you is the sound of tractors on the field, but then a road cutting across the countryside spoils the peace. Shortly afterwards you cross the Swanston Burn which, despite its modest proportions, was one of the causes of the development of Swanston, since it provided water for the village.

From here the road begins to climb gently out of the small valley between the main road which is a result of glacial erosion in the Ice Age. Through the trees you can see glimpses of whitewashed cottages, although most of the village is well screened by trees. Pass the farmhouse buildings and continue on until you come to the car park. Keeping on the road, bear round to the right and cross over the'burn. Gradually chimney pots begin to appear and soon the road arrives at a U-shaped collection of cottages nestling under the hill. Single-storeyed with slate roofs they present a very attractive picture.

Walk past the cottages and across the burn can be seen the White House, once the village school and now a private house. It is a handsome sight with its white-washed walls, slate roof, and slightly bowed front surrounded by a well-tended garden. Continue on the road to the right and you soon come to the climax of the village, two rows of thatched cottages either side of the green. These were built in the 18th century but restored to a high standard by the Corporation in 1959–62. The result is extremely picturesque with the thatched roofs topping white-washed walls which are decorated by grey surrounds around the windows.

In Stevenson's day the cottages were quite simple containing only one room and earth for a floor, but the author leaves us in no doubt as to how house-proud their inhabitants were: 'models of neatness, beds with patchwork covers, shelves with willow pattern plates, the floors and table bright with scrubbing . . . and the very kettle polished like silver'. Judging by the exteriors of the cottages the new inhabitants are just as careful, in fact the cottages look almost too manicured to be real. Each cottage has its own carefully swept gravel path and stone setts surround the green, while behind the houses one can glimpse well-kept gardens.

At the top of the village green is a seat dedicated to another literary figure, Edwin Muir, who is described as 'Poet, Novelist, Essayist' who liked to 'meditate and linger here'. Many people will be tempted to do likewise. Swanston truly is, as it has been described, 'a fold in the lap of the Pentlands'. Ahead is the peak of Caerketton Hill at 1,568 feet high while slightly to the right is Allermuir Hill, 1,618 feet high.

Through the gate is the last cottage in the village, in the same style as the others around the green. Turn round and go back towards the other cottages, and in the far distance the lion-like shape of Arthur's Seat can be detected. Walk back down the path to the right of the burn from where you can get a clearer view of the White House, and also of a grey deserted building you may have seen as you walked up. This was once thought to have been a grange of Whitekirk Abbey but this is now beginning to seem unlikely. The present building, which is an old farmhouse, dates from the 18th century and must once have been quite impressive with its crow-stepped gables. Now unfortunately it is unoccupied, and being allowed to decay.

This path brings you back to the car park. To the left is the clubhouse of the Swanston Golf Course and just below this a bungalow, the only modern house to be built in the old village.

To get to Swanston Cottage, Stevenson's old home, go back down the road and turn left just past the farm buildings. These were built in the early 19th century and present an attractive front onto the road with gables built over arches which lead into a courtyard. The road leads up to a gateway which is the entrance to Swanston Cottage. Just inside is the cottage of 'Cummy's'. This was Alison Cunningham, nanny to Robert Louis Stevenson and referred to by him as his 'second mother and first wife'. The author dedicated his *A Child's Garden of Verses* to 'Cummy' who came to Swanston with the Stevensons and stayed there until 1813, long after the departure of the family.

Above the door is an inscription of '1880 A.C. 1893', recording her stay in the cottage.

Unfortunately for Stevenson fans the drive to Swanston Cottage is strictly private. To obtain a sight of the cottage we therefore have to walk round the track to the left by the side of the golf course. From here you can see across to the house and can realise that Swanston Cottage is a cottage in name only for it is in fact an impressively large house.

Swanston Cottage was orginally built in 1761 in connection with the waterworks using the spring just below, and soon became a grand house, where as Robert Louis Stevenson describes, 'purple magistrates relaxed themselves from the pursuit of municipal ambition'. The grounds were extensive and divided into three gardens, the Rose Garden, the Quarry Garden and the Queen Anne Garden. The house was extended in the 19th century before Stevenson's parents hired the house for the summer in 1867, hoping that the quiet country air would improve Stevenson's always fragile constitution and delicate health. The author fell in love with the spot and the family came here right up to 1880.

From this vantage point it is not easy to see the house clearly especially as most of the house projects a long way back from the front part which we can see. We must therefore content ourselves with Stevenson's own very graphic if rather fanciful description of what it looked like in his time as it described it in his novel, *St Ives*:

The cottage was a little quaint place of many rough cast gables and grey roofs. It had something of the air of a rambling infinitesimal cathedral, the body of it rising in the midst 2 storeys high, with a steep pitched roof and sending out upon all hands (as it were chapter-houses, chapels and transepts) one-storeyed and dwarfish projections. To add to this appearance it was grotesquely decorated with crockets and gargoyles, ravished from some mediaeval church.

It is believed that the mediaeval church in question was none other than St Giles' Church in the High Street in Edinburgh.

Walk towards the road again and as you walk it is quite probable that you may see a shepherd tending his flock in the same way that John Todd, the Swanston Shepherd, did in Stevenson's *Pentland Essays*. Another old villager, Robert Young, the old Scotch Gardener, is also immortalised in this collection, and it seems that Swanston not only provided the young Stevenson with country air but also inspiration for his writing.

Turn left onto Swanston Road and walk away from the village. As you look back you can see the curious T shaped wood behind the cottages which are now out of view again. This was planted in 1760 by the Trotter family who owned the land supposedly as a memorial to their descendants who had died in battle. Another theory has been put forward to explain its T shape. It is suggested, perhaps maliciously, that the wood was planted in a T formation to assert Trotter's domination over the land after he had been defeated by the Edinburgh Corporation in a dispute about the use of the springs. Each theory sounds rather unlikely particularly as the wood is actually built in the form of a Greek Cross although it does look like a T when seen at a distance.

Walk back to the main road and firmly into the 20th century once more.

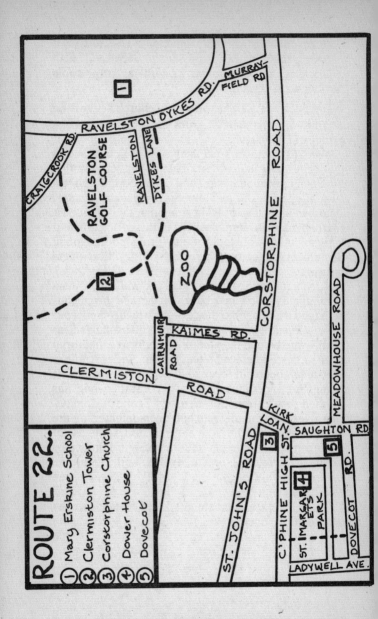

ROUTE 22.

1 Mary Erskine School
2 Clermiston Tower
3 Corstorphine Church
4 Dower House
5 Dovecot

RAVELSTON DYKES RD.
MURRAY-FIELD RD.
CRAIGCROOK RD.
RAVELSTON DYKES
RAVELSTON GOLF COURSE
RAVELSTON DYKES LANE
CORSTORPHINE ROAD
ZOO
CAIRNMUIR ROAD
KAIMES RD.
CLERMISTON ROAD
MEADOWHOUSE ROAD
KIRK LOAN
SAUGHTON RD.
ST. JOHN'S ROAD
C'PHINE HIGH ST.
ST. MARGARETS PARK
DOVECOT RD.
LADYWELL AVE.

Route 22

CORSTORPHINE HILL AND VILLAGE

This walk is really in two halves. The first part takes you over Corstorphine Hill, one of the loveliest spots in Edinburgh, and the other explores the old village of Corstorphine. Each part can be done separately although together they make a very satisfying walk.

We begin our ascent of Corstorphine Hill from Ravelston Dykes, with the Mary Erskine School for Girls on your left. Part of the school buildings are housed in New Ravelston House, and the remnants of old Ravelston House stand within its grounds. The original gateway of the old house still stands as does a crow-stepped tower built in 1622. Above the door are the initials of the first owners, George Foulis and his wife, Janet Bannatyne. New Ravelston House, built in 1791, is said to have provided the inspiration for Tullyveolan in Sir Walter Scott's novel *Waverley*.

Beyond the school take the path just past Ravelston Dykes Lane which leads up the hill to the right beside the golf course. This develops into a lovely peaceful wooded walk lined on the right by old lampstands. As you climb look back to the right to see the sea. We soon come to the viewpoint known as 'Rest and be Thankful' where David Balfour, the hero of Robert Louis Stevenson's novel, *Kidnapped*, took his leave from the Jacobite, Alan Breck. To the left, Arthur's Seat can be clearly seen in the distance. Climbing further you may be surprised to come across deer and other wild animals, safely fenced off. You are now walking round the boundary of Edinburgh Zoo which, amongst other attributes, claims to have the largest colony of penguins outside Antarctica.

Keeping the zoo boundary on your left, you eventually come to steep steps. Descend these and go straight across at the intersection of paths. The land dips into a wide open bowl where seats have been thoughtfully provided for weary feet. Cross this ground and mount more steps which take you up to a stone tower, now all boarded up. This is Clermiston or Corstorphine Tower which was erected in 1871 to mark the centenary of the birth of Sir Walter Scott. To the right and in front of the tower you will find the ruins of a beacon tower. This is one of many towers where bale-fires were used to signal messages from the hills along the East Coast to those inland.

Walk back the way you came. Straight in front of you there is a marvellous view of the Pentland Hills, particularly stunning if the sun is catching the peaks. When you reach the crossroads again turn to the right with the zoo boundary on your left. This path soon brings you out to a road. Follow Cairnmuir Road, past an elegantly turreted house set in sumptuous gardens, to the T junction with Clermiston Road. Turn left and walk down the hill to join St John's Road. This area used to form the high village of Corstorphine which was separate from the low village until the 20th century.

To get to the old low village turn immediately left into Kirk Loan, a narrow lane running to the left of a new shopping precinct. Kirk Loan, as its name suggests, soon brings you out at Corstorphine's old church. There has been some form of church on this spot since the 12th century when St Mary's Church, belonging to the Abbey of Holyrood, was built. In 1337 Sir Adam Forrester, laird of Corstorphine, built a small chapel alongside the Norman one. This was later extended by his son, John Forrester, to form the nucleus of the present church with the old chapel as the chancel. In 1828 the church suffered a heavy-handed programme of restoration and alteration resulting in damage to the original nave. In 1905 the church was given another, but this time more sensitive, face-lift.

At the end of the day, the church is still very attractive in a marvellous setting in front of the Pentland Hills. It has several unusual features such as the massive roof of stone slabs and a thick tower with a stone spire. To get a better view of these, and to gain entrance to the church you need to walk most of the way round it. As you do so look up on the wall nearest you to see the small lamp under the roof. In the days when Corstorphine was situated on a boggy marshland at the end of a loch, people travelling at night were often dependent for their safety on this lamp. Now lit by electricity it no longer has this vital part to play.

The church itself is entered through fine iron gates, decorated with thistles, and inside it contains several statues, one of which, depicting an armoured knight, is said to represent Sir Adam Forrester, the founder of the original chapel. The gallery has rather a grisly story attached to it. A girl suspected of being a witch, a crime for which she would be burnt to death, hanged herself in the gallery while the session below discussed her case. The judges were disturbed from their deliberations by the ringing of the bell which the weight of the poor girl's body had caused to toll.

Leave the church and bear round to the right into the High Street, the heart of the low village of Corstorphine. There are several suggestions for the name of the village, each of which is quite fanciful. Some say that the village is named after Torphin, a famous Saxon hero, others that it comes from its Gaelic meaning which is roughly, 'white mist that lies in the hollow', which is seen as apt to its geographical situation. Using a French translation, Corstorphine becomes 'Croix d'or fin', possibly after a gold church treasure. Whatever the truth of the matter, a cross of five trees was always recognised as the village centre. Unfortunately this cross was destroyed when the village school was transferred to its present site in 1819. The old school, a small thatched cottage, used to stand on the site of Albyn Cottage to your right.

The cross, which probably stood at the entrance to St Margaret's Park on your left, was a centre of market activity selling the produce of the surrounding rich soil which had been reclaimed from the marsh. But it was at the other end of the village to the east, at the Tron tree, that Corstorphine cream was sold. This cream, rather like Devonshire cream, was very popular in the 18th century. Visitors would come and stay and reputedly take the cream away in barrels.

By the 18th century in fact Corstorphine had become a popular tourist centre for the city dwellers from Edinburgh. Corstorphine cream was not the only attraction, for there were also mineral wells boasting health-giving powers. The wells were so popular that special coaches ran from Edinburgh carrying passengers who wished to taste 'its salubrious waters'. The wells no longer exist although they are remembered in the name of Ladywell Road which is a continuation of the High Street.

Go in through the park gates and straight in front of you is the Dower House which was built between 1660–1670 by the Forrester family. As its name indicates, this was the Dower House built to accompany the old castle which once existed on the other side of the park. In fact it is thought the drive which you are now standing on once led to this castle. At the time of the Jacobite rising in 1745 the inhabitants of the Dower House gave hospitality to the Young Pretender, Prince Charles, during his onslaught on Edinburgh. The house itself is a handsome building with crow-stepped gables, and enjoys a fine backcloth of the Pentland Hills.

Turn right onto the path parallel to the High Street and then left, and walk down to the exit gate. Turn left into Dovecot Road. As you near the end of the road you can see why this road is so called for to the left is a large circular dovecot. This is the only evidence left of Corstorphine Castle bult in the 14th century by the Forrester family, but which was destroyed, save for the dovecot, by the 18th century. The dovecot itself was built in the 16th century and contains more than 1,000 pigeon-holes although unfortunately as it is now shut up we cannot see these.

This building does not proclaim the nature-loving quality of the Corstorphine lords, for these dovecots had a very practical purpose which probably explains their long survival. As John Galt graphicly describes in his *Last of the Lairds*, 'our ancestors kindly provided convenient places where their doves, returning heavy and over-fed with foraging in their neighbours' cornfields, might repose and fatten for spit or pie in unmolested equanimity'.

Behind the dovecot are the offices of the Edinburgh Tapestry Company, situated in Dovecot Studios, which continue to produce beautiful handworked tapestries. To the left as the road bends round is a fine old sycamore tree. In times gone by this tree used to be haunted by a White Lady, carrying a bloodstained sword, wailing and bemoaning her fate. This was the ghost of Christine Nimmo who in 1679 stabbed Lord James Forrester, her former lover, for making fun of her, and was later hanged for her crime. The tree itself is believed to have been grown from a seed brought by a monk from the Holy Land in the 15th century.

Follow Sycamore Terrace which turns into Saughton Road, and take the second right into Kirk Loan which takes you out of the village.

ROUTE 23.

① Henry Mackenzie's Cottage
② Colinton Church
③ Redhall Mill
④ Merchiston Castle School
⑤ Ruins of Colinton Castle
⑥ Gillespie's Mill
⑦ West Mill

COLINTON MAINS DRIVE

PATIE'S RD.

COLINTON ROAD

REDFORD ROAD

WESTGARTH AVE.

WEIR

WATER OF LEITH

DELL RD.

SPYLAW ST.

BRIDGE ROAD

WOODHALL ROAD

GILLESPIE ROAD

WEIR

SPYLAW PARK

WEST MILL RD.

Route 23

COLINTON

Colinton with its river, the Water of Leith, used to be a thriving milling community. Now it has become absorbed into the residential spread of Edinburgh and yet it still has, at its heart, an old village providing beautiful walks by the wooded banks of the river.

Enter Colinton Village by branching off from Colinton Road into Bridge Road, just opposite Westgarth Avenue. This avenue used to be the end of the tram line from the city centre until it ceased to run in 1955.

At the top of Bridge Road on the right at the traffic lights, is a small cottage sunk from the level of the road. A plaque to the left of the building tells you that this was the home of Henry Mackenzie from 1745 to 1831. Mackenzie achieved fame with his sentimental novel, *The Man of Feeling*, published in 1771. The cottage was thatched in Mackenzie's day and although the house is now nearly derelict, there is sufficient vegetation on the roof to allow you to imagine its former thatched appearance.

Walk down the slope a little way and take the steps pointing towards the Parish Church and immediately you are away from the bustle of the shops. Passing stone cottages to the right you come to the bottom where you really feel you are in a village, and can now begin to appreciate James Ballantine's description of Colinton in *The Miller of Deanhaugh* with 'its romantic valley, its line of cottages embodied in the hollows . . .'

To the left of you is a street of distinctive and very attractive cottages, but we will explore these later. Instead turn right towards the church and cross the river. After you have walked over the bridge turn towards the cemetery on the river bank, and instead of the tranquil scene which now meets your eye, imagine instead the thriving and bustling activity of the mills of which once stood here. If you can imagine that there were once 80 mills in 10 miles of river you can begin to understand quite how industrial this part once was.

Now the river, shallow and full of boulders, looks of little use but once it powered Kirkland Mill, erected here in 1585 to produce lint which was a product of flax and part of the process of producing linen. Later the mills were used to produce snuff and tobacco and then, from 1870–1916 for the manufacture of 'mill-boards', which were the boards used in bookbinding. Slightly further down the river was another mill, Hole or Holm Mill, which was demolished in 1870. The road to the right takes you down to the old Manse but since it is in private hands we cannot investigate it, but must content ourselves with a view of the house from further up the road. Walk up to Colinton Church further on the right which is in a superb position in a hollow by the river.

Enter the churchyard and stop on the left just in front of the porch. The long coffin-shaped, metallic object which you can see is a mortsafe. These were used to prevent recently buried bodies being dug up by 'grave-snatchers', to be sold to doctors for dissecting purposes. Such was the danger of this happening that these safes were made and placed on the grave after a person had been buried, and only when the body was judged to be sufficiently decayed so as to be no good for medical purposes, was the mortsafe removed. At one time there were at least 3 or 4 of these objects which weighed one ton and therefore, one imagines, must have been quite effective.

A board inside the porch of the church gives an

account of its history. The original parish church was founded in 1095 further down the river where Hailes House now stands. At this time one of the sons of King Malcolm of Canmore gave the church certain lands known as Hale or Hailes, and for a long time the village bore this name. The original church was dedicated in 1248 but then seems to have 'disappeared' around 1260 and was finally finished off for good during the invasion by the Earl of Hertford in 1544–45.

The present church was originally built in 1641 although it was substantially reconstructed in 1908. Soon after the building of the church the village began to be called, 'Collingtoun' although no-one seems to be able to explain why this was. In the 18th century it took on its present title of Colinton.

Wander around the churchyard to see the fascinating array of tombstones, many with a skull and crossbones on them. To the left of the church is the tomb of James Gillespie, a local snuff manufacturer and benefactor of Edinburgh. Next door is the tombstone of the Reverend Lewis Balfour who was Minister of Colinton for nearly 37 years between 1823–1860. If you go back to the road and bear round to the right you can look back to see the Manse which was once the home of Rev. Balfour.

Rev. Balfour was the maternal grandfather of the author Robert Louis Stevenson, who was in fact baptised Robert Lewis Balfour Stevenson but later dropped the 'Balfour' part and changed the spelling of 'Lewis'. The young author spent many hours of his childhood in the Manse and it is believed that the Manse's garden provided the setting for *A Child's Garden of Verses*. Robert Louis Stevenson records how 'this lawn was my favourite playground . . . in the great laurel at the corner I have often laid "perdu" with a toy-gun in my hand, waiting for a herd of antelopes to file past me down the carriage drive, and waiting (need I add) in vain'. In a foretaste of *Treasure Island*, the young author fantasised that he was a pirate up a tree and that the 'wicket [gate] is the harbour and the garden is the shore'. The Manse itself was built in 1783, and added to in 1807 and, as we look back to the sight of it by the river, we can well imagine that it was, 'a well-beloved house, with its image fondly dwelt upon by many travellers'.

Dell Road brings you down into Colinton Dell and a beautiful walk by the Water of Leith. Here we can see how more of Ballantine's description is borne out: 'its sylvan pathways threading the mazes of wood, deep, deep down in the beautiful dell'. Again this area was once alive with the sound of mills: as Robert Louis Stevenson said, 'there is the sound of water and the sound of mills – the wheel and the dam singing their alternative strain'. Now as the river winds its way amongst the thick woods there is little to disturb the peace and beauty of the scene. Unfortunately a stone wall impedes your view a little further down but we soon come out again at the weir and can see that the name which the village finally ended up with was very suitable for Colinton means 'the homestead beside the weir in the valley of the hills'.

If you wish to see a mill which still remains, although not in use for milling, cross the river and walk on the path between the main river and the stream or mill-lade which once provided power for the wheel. After a little way you have to cross the stream and climb up wooden steps out of the dell. Below, you can see the remnants of Redhall Mill. This began work in 1718 and in its time was used for milling paper, sawdust and barley. Nearby was another mill, Kate's Mill, working as early as 1540 which was burnt down in 1890 and is now only remembered by the name of the house on the spot.

To continue the rest of this walk retrace your steps back to the weir. On the right are the remains of Colinton Castle and the building of Colinton House. Unfortunately these are now in the private grounds of Merchiston Castle School and hidden from view. Colinton House was built between 1801–1806 for Sir William Forbes, a famous Edinburgh banker. Colinton Castle which is now completely ruined was built for Sir James Foulis in the 16th century. At one time this family owned nearly the whole of Colinton Parish, then stretching over some six villages or settlements. In 1790 the Castle passed into the hands of Sir William Forbes until Colinton House was built to replace it. The Castle was the setting for *The Open Door*, a ghost story by Mrs Oliphant.

Cross the river once more and climb the steps to the right, and at the top turn left onto a wide track. You are now on an old railway track and, as if to confirm this, you soon pass under a long tunnel which has had a picture of a train painted on its left-hand side. The railway line used to serve the paper mills situated all the way along the river to Balerno. This tunnel brings you out the other side of Bridge Road. Take the steps to the left into Spylaw Park.

A collection of millstones bordering round a house indicate that the stone building by the river was once a mill. This house, originally built in 1650 but altered in the 18th century, was the home and working quarters of James Gillespie. It was here that the snuff was ground which made Gillespie wealthy and thus led to Gillespie's bequests to the city in the form of money for schools. In 1779 Gillespie added a house frontage to the 17th century mill situated at the back and thus he was able to live above the mill which he owned. Tales are told of how he used to supervise the mill shortly before his death in 1793, attired only in an old blanket and night-cap which were both thickly encrusted with snuff. The house itself is very attractive with a double staircase leading up to the front door and an iron balcony running along the right-side of the house.

Follow the boundary of the park three-quarters of the way round and leave the park on the right to rejoin the old railway line. Cross the river and on the left you can see the offices of the Forth River Purification Board. These are housed in one of the West Mills which was the centre of Scott's Porage Oats production until 1971. These mills were built in 1800 by Thomas King and used as grain mills, until one was demolished the other turned over to its present use.

Rejoin the river path by the gate to the right which signposts you to Juniper Green. The path soon crosses the river again at another weir. These weirs were used to increase the head of the river so it had sufficient power to work the mills situated further down stream. At the crossroads a few yards further down, turn right up the road. As you near the top of this hill you can look across to the right to see the Pentland Hills.

Walk back along the right-hand side of Gillespie Road looking across to West Mill and Spylaw Park. Cross the river on Bridge Road which is obviously aptly named, and turn left down Spylaw Street. You can now see clearly the cottages which we glimpsed before. These were acquired in 1799 by the Merchant Company of Edinburgh under the will of James Gillespie. They form a very attractive row with their white-washed walls and tiled roofs. Notice the unusual projecting porches which are supported on wooden beams on the houses towards the bottom of the road.

As you near the foot of the hill you can hear the sound of the river once more. From here you can take the steps back up to Bridge Road and conclude the walk.

GLOSSARY

Architectural Terms

Apse:
: Semi-circular or many-sided recess which in a church is usually situated at the eastern end.

Astragal:
: Usually refers to a small semi-circular moulding in stone but it also describes the narrow bars which separate panes of glass in a window, as in the New Town.

Casement:
: Window which is hinged on its edges so it can open either inwards or outwards.

Chancel:
: Eastern part of church used by the choir or clergy.

Corinthian:
: One of the orders of classical architecture. Characterised by ornate leaf decorations (acanthus, olive or laurel leaves) at the top of the columns.

Crow-stepped Gable:
: A gable whose sides are not straight but are cut to resemble steps, (also called corbie-step).

Cruciform:
: In the shape of a cross.

Doric:
: Earliest order of classical architecture and the plainest with no decoration at the top of the columns. Greek Doric differs from Roman Doric in having no base to its columns.

Dormer (window):
: Upright window which projects from a sloping roof – usually at the top or attic of a house.

Dutch Gable:	A curved or shaped gable topped by a triangular portion of stone or *pediment*.
Finial:	The ornament crowning a pinnacle, spire or, most commonly in the New Town, railings. Often in the shape of an arrowhead, urn or fleur-de-lis.
Gable:	Triangular portion of wall at the end of ridged roof.
Hammerbeam Roof:	Roof formed by horizontal beams projecting from opposite walls. The beams do not meet in the middle but are supported on arched brackets.
Ionic:	An order of classical architecture which is characterised by scroll-like ornamentation at the top of the columns.
Lintel:	Horizontal timber or stone over a door or window which bridges a gap.
Pantile:	Roof tile cut cross-wise so it is curved into an S shape.
Pediment:	Triangular part crowning a building. In classical architecture it is usually above a set of columns and supports the roof.
Pilaster:	Rectangular column which projects slightly from wall. Used as a form of decoration.
Portico:	Covered entrance to a building supported by columns.